Small Business, Big Results

How Digital Marketing Can Help You Build Your Brand and Boost Your Bottom

Tyler Carter

Foreward

As the digital landscape continues to evolve, small businesses must adapt to the changing times and embrace digital marketing. In today's market, it is no longer enough to rely solely on traditional marketing methods. The advent of social media, email marketing, search engine optimization (SEO), pay-per-click (PPC) advertising, content marketing, influencer marketing, and affiliate marketing has made it easier than ever for small businesses to reach their target audiences and achieve their business goals.

This book is an essential guide for small businesses seeking to implement effective digital marketing strategies. In Chapter 1, readers will learn about the various digital marketing channels available and the advantages of using them, including cost-effectiveness, targeted audience, measurable results, increased brand awareness, competitive advantage, increased customer conversion, greater flexibility and adaptability, better customer insights, greater reach and visibility, and improved customer retention.

In Chapter 2, readers will discover the importance of understanding their audience, how to identify their target market, conduct market research, develop buyer personas, analyze competitors, use data and analytics, and create customer personas. Chapter 3 focuses on website development and optimization, including the importance of a user-friendly design, mobile optimization, branding, content strategy, website functionality, social media integration, analytics, and search engine optimization (SEO) strategies.

Chapter 4 delves into social media marketing, including the role of social media in digital marketing, how to choose the right platforms, create a content strategy, engage with your audience, measure your results, and stay up-to-date with trends. Chapter 5 explores the importance of email marketing for small businesses, including how to build a targeted email list, create personalized messages, use a clear and compelling subject line, include a clear call-to-action (CTA), and measure results.

Chapter 6 introduces pay-per-click (PPC) advertising, including the benefits of PPC advertising for small businesses, the Google Ads and Facebook Ads platforms, and how to create and manage PPC campaigns. Chapter 7 focuses on content marketing, including the importance of content marketing, types of content, content creation and management strategies, and measuring content marketing success.

In Chapter 8, readers will learn about influencer marketing, including the definition and importance of influencer marketing, how to find the right influencers for your brand, build relationships with influencers, and measure influencer marketing success. Chapter 9 introduces affiliate marketing, including the definition and importance of affiliate marketing, how to set up an affiliate program, find and recruit affiliates, and measure affiliate marketing success.

Chapter 10 emphasizes the importance of analytics and measurement, including tools such as Google Analytics and other tools, setting goals and KPIs, and measuring digital marketing success and ROI. Chapter 11 guides readers on how to create a digital marketing plan, including setting objectives and goals, developing a budget, creating a timeline and action plan.

Finally, Chapter 12 provides best practices for small business digital marketing, including consistency in branding and messaging, staying up-to-date with trends and technologies, engaging with customers and responding to feedback, and continuous testing and optimization.

In conclusion, this book is a must-read for small business owners and entrepreneurs looking to gain a competitive edge in the digital marketplace. The insights and strategies provided will help them leverage digital marketing channels to reach their target audience, achieve their business goals, and stay ahead of the competition.

Summary

Chapter 1: Introduction

What is digital marketing?

Digital marketing is a type of marketing that uses digital channels and technologies to promote and advertise products or services. The goal of digital marketing is to reach potential customers where they are spending most of their time: online. Digital marketing can encompass a wide range of tactics, including social media marketing, email marketing, search engine optimization (SEO), pay-per-click (PPC) advertising, content marketing, influencer marketing, and more.

One of the main benefits of digital marketing is that it offers cost-effective ways to reach a large audience. Many digital marketing tactics, such as social media and email marketing, are often more affordable than traditional advertising methods, such as print or TV ads. This makes digital marketing especially appealing to small businesses or companies with limited marketing budgets.

Another advantage of digital marketing is that it allows businesses to target specific audiences based on demographics, interests, and behaviors. For example, through social media advertising, a business can target users who have expressed an interest in their products or services, or who fit a specific demographic profile. This ensures that the business's message reaches the right people, increasing the chances of conversion.

Digital marketing also provides businesses with valuable insights into customer behavior and preferences. By tracking and measuring the effectiveness of their campaigns, businesses can gain insights into which tactics are working and which are not. This information can be used to optimize future campaigns and improve overall marketing strategy.

To give you a more detailed understanding of some of the key digital marketing tactics, let's explore a few examples:

Social media marketing: This involves using social media platforms, such as Facebook, Instagram, and Twitter, to promote products or services, build brand awareness, and engage with customers. Social media marketing can include organic tactics, such as creating and sharing content, as well as paid advertising, such as running targeted ads.

Email marketing: This involves sending promotional messages or newsletters to a list of subscribers via email. Email marketing can be an effective way to build relationships with customers, promote products or services, and drive sales. It's important to ensure that email campaigns are personalized, engaging, and relevant to the recipient.

Search engine optimization (SEO): This involves optimizing a website and its content to rank higher in search engine results pages (SERPs). By improving website content, using targeted keywords, and building high-quality backlinks, businesses can increase their visibility in search engine results, driving more organic traffic to their website.

Pay-per-click (PPC) advertising: This involves placing ads on search engines, social media platforms, or other websites and paying a fee each time a user clicks on the ad. PPC advertising can be a highly targeted way to reach potential customers, and it offers measurable results, allowing businesses to track their return on investment (ROI).

Content marketing: This involves creating and distributing valuable, relevant, and engaging content to attract and retain a target audience. Content marketing can include blog posts, videos, infographics, podcasts, and more. By creating high-quality content that addresses customer needs or pain points, businesses can build trust, establish themselves as industry experts, and ultimately drive sales.

Influencer marketing: This involves partnering with individuals who have a large following on social media or other platforms, and who can promote a product or service to their audience. Influencer marketing can be a highly effective way to reach new audiences and build brand awareness, especially for businesses in industries such as fashion, beauty, or food.

These are just a few examples of the many digital marketing tactics that businesses can use to reach and engage with customers online. By using a mix of tactics, and continually testing and optimizing campaigns, businesses can build a strong digital marketing strategy that drives results and helps them achieve their goals.

Why digital marketing is essential for small businesses?

Digital marketing is essential for small businesses because it offers cost-effective ways to reach a large audience, compete with larger companies, and drive sales and revenue. In today's digital age, consumers rely more on the internet and mobile devices for information and purchasing decisions, making digital marketing an increasingly important aspect of any business's marketing strategy.

One of the main benefits of digital marketing for small businesses is cost-effectiveness. Many digital marketing tactics, such as social media marketing and email marketing, are often more affordable than traditional advertising methods, such as print or TV ads. This makes digital marketing especially appealing to small businesses or companies with limited marketing budgets.

Another advantage of digital marketing is that it allows small businesses to reach a larger audience than they might otherwise be able to. By using digital channels such as social media, search engines, or email, small businesses can reach potential customers across a wide geographic area, regardless of their physical location. This can help small businesses expand their reach, compete with larger companies, and establish themselves as industry leaders.

Digital marketing also allows small businesses to target specific audiences based on demographics, interests, and behaviors. For example, a small business selling eco-friendly products can use social media advertising to target users who have expressed an interest in sustainability, or who fit a specific demographic profile. This ensures that the business's message reaches the right people, increasing the chances of conversion.

Additionally, digital marketing provides small businesses with valuable insights into customer behavior and preferences. By tracking and measuring the effectiveness of their campaigns, small businesses can gain insights into which tactics are working and which are not. This information can be used to optimize future campaigns and improve overall marketing strategy, ultimately driving sales and revenue.

Digital marketing also provides small businesses with the opportunity to build relationships with customers, foster loyalty, and encourage repeat business. By using tactics such as email marketing or social media, small businesses can engage with customers in real-time, responding to questions or feedback and providing personalized support. This can help to build trust, establish a positive reputation, and increase customer satisfaction.

Another advantage of digital marketing for small businesses is its scalability. Digital marketing tactics can be adjusted and optimized based on business needs, budgets, or growth goals. For example, a small business might start with a basic social media presence and gradually increase their efforts as they gain more followers and engagement. This makes digital marketing an ideal option for businesses looking to grow and expand over time.

Finally, digital marketing is essential for small businesses because it can provide a competitive advantage. By using a mix of tactics, and continually testing and optimizing campaigns, small businesses can build a strong digital marketing strategy that differentiates them from their competitors. This can help small businesses stand out in crowded markets, build a loyal customer base, and ultimately, drive revenue growth.

In summary, digital marketing is essential for small businesses because it offers a cost-effective, targeted, and scalable way to reach potential customers, build relationships, and drive sales and revenue. By leveraging digital marketing tactics effectively, small businesses can establish themselves as industry leaders, compete with larger companies, and achieve their business goals.

Advantages and benefits of digital marketing for small businesses

Digital marketing offers numerous advantages and benefits for small businesses, making it an essential aspect of any modern marketing strategy. Here are some of the key advantages and benefits of digital marketing for small businesses:

Cost-effectiveness: Digital marketing tactics, such as social media marketing, email marketing, and content marketing, are often more affordable than traditional advertising methods. This makes digital marketing especially appealing to small businesses with limited marketing budgets.

Targeted audience: Digital marketing allows small businesses to target specific audiences based on demographics, interests, and behaviors. By using tactics such as social media advertising or search engine marketing, small businesses can ensure that their message reaches the right people, increasing the chances of conversion.

Measurable results: Digital marketing provides small businesses with valuable insights into customer behavior and preferences. By tracking and measuring the effectiveness of their campaigns, small businesses can gain insights into which tactics are working and which are not. This information can be used to optimize future campaigns and improve overall marketing strategy.

Increased brand awareness: Digital marketing can help small businesses build brand awareness and establish themselves as industry leaders. By using tactics such as content marketing or social media, small businesses can create valuable and engaging content that resonates with their target audience, increasing brand recognition and loyalty.

Increased engagement: Digital marketing allows small businesses to engage with customers in real-time, fostering loyalty and customer satisfaction. By using tactics such as social media or email marketing, small businesses can respond to questions or feedback, provide personalized support, and build relationships with their customers.

Competitive advantage: Digital marketing provides small businesses with a competitive advantage by helping them stand out in crowded markets. By using a mix of tactics, small businesses can differentiate themselves from their competitors, build a loyal customer base, and ultimately, drive revenue growth.

Increased customer conversion: Digital marketing can help small businesses convert potential customers into paying customers. By using tactics such as search engine optimization, pay-per-click advertising, or email marketing, small businesses can attract customers who are actively searching for their products or services, increasing the chances of conversion.

Greater flexibility and adaptability: Digital marketing allows small businesses to adjust their marketing strategies based on their needs, budgets, or growth goals. By using tactics such as social media or content marketing, small businesses can experiment with different approaches, test new ideas, and adapt to changing market conditions.

Better customer insights: Digital marketing provides small businesses with valuable insights into customer behavior and preferences. By tracking and analyzing data such as website traffic, social media engagement, or email open rates, small businesses can gain insights into their customers' needs, preferences, and pain points. This information can be used to create more personalized and effective marketing campaigns.

Greater reach and visibility: Digital marketing can help small businesses reach a wider audience than they might otherwise be able to. By using tactics such as social media advertising or search engine marketing, small businesses can reach potential customers across a wide geographic area, increasing their visibility and exposure.

Improved customer retention: Digital marketing can help small businesses build long-term relationships with their customers. By using tactics such as email marketing or social media, small businesses can keep in touch with their customers, provide ongoing value, and encourage repeat business.

In summary, digital marketing provides small businesses with numerous advantages and benefits, including cost-effectiveness, targeted audience, measurable results, increased brand awareness and engagement, competitive advantage, customer conversion, flexibility and adaptability, customer insights, greater reach and visibility, and improved customer retention. By using digital marketing tactics effectively, small businesses can establish themselves as industry leaders, compete with larger companies, and ultimately, achieve their business goals.

Chapter 2: Understanding your audience

Identifying your target audience

Identifying your target audience is a crucial step in developing a successful marketing strategy. Knowing who your ideal customers are and what they want can help you create more targeted and effective marketing messages, products, and services. Here are some key steps for identifying your target audience:

The first step is to conduct market research. This can involve analyzing data such as customer demographics, buying patterns, and online behavior. By gaining insights into your target audience's needs, behaviors, and preferences, you can better understand their pain points and motivations.

The next step is to develop buyer personas. A buyer persona is a fictional representation of your ideal customer. By creating detailed buyer personas, you can better understand your target audience's pain points, motivations, and behaviors, and tailor your marketing messages accordingly.

In addition to demographics, it's also important to consider psychographic factors such as personality, values, and lifestyle when identifying your target audience. These factors can help you create more targeted and effective marketing campaigns that resonate with your ideal customers.

Analyzing your competitors can also provide valuable insights into their target audience and the strategies they are using to reach them. This can help you identify gaps in the market and opportunities to differentiate your business.

Using data and analytics is another critical step in identifying your target audience. By tracking and measuring the effectiveness of your marketing campaigns, you can gain insights into your target audience's behaviors and preferences. This can help you adjust your strategies and tactics to better meet their needs.

Testing and refining your marketing strategies over time is essential for identifying your target audience. By experimenting with different approaches and analyzing the results, you can refine your target audience, messaging, and tactics to optimize your marketing efforts.

To further expand on the process of identifying your target audience, let's take a closer look at each of these steps:

Conduct market research: There are many different methods for conducting market research, including surveys, focus groups, and analyzing data from customer transactions and online behavior. The goal of market research is to gain a better understanding of your target audience's needs, preferences, and behaviors, and to identify trends and patterns that can inform your marketing strategy.

Develop buyer personas: A buyer persona is a detailed profile of your ideal customer that includes information such as age, gender, income, education level, and job title. You can also include more detailed information such as hobbies, interests, and personality traits. The goal of developing buyer personas is to create a clear picture of who your ideal customers are, and to tailor your marketing messages and tactics to meet their specific needs and preferences.

Consider psychographic factors: In addition to demographics, psychographic factors such as personality, values, and lifestyle can also play a role in identifying your target audience. For example, if you sell environmentally-friendly products, you might target customers who are passionate about sustainability and social responsibility.

Analyze competitors: Analyzing your competitors can provide valuable insights into their target audience and the strategies they are using to reach them. Look at their marketing messages, social media presence, and advertising campaigns to see who they are targeting and how they are positioning themselves in the market.

Use data and analytics: Data and analytics can provide valuable insights into your target audience's behaviors and preferences, and can help you track and measure the effectiveness of your marketing campaigns. For example, you can use website analytics to see which pages on your site are the most popular, or use social media analytics to track engagement and audience demographics.

Test and refine: Testing and refining your marketing strategies over time is essential for identifying your target audience. Experiment with different messaging and tactics, and analyze the results to see which approaches are most effective. Use this information to refine your target audience and tailor your marketing efforts to better meet their needs and preferences.

In summary, identifying your target audience is a complex process that involves conducting market research, developing buyer personas, considering psychographic factors, analyzing competitors, using data and analytics, and testing and refining over time. By understanding your ideal customers and tailoring your marketing efforts to meet their needs and preferences, you can create more effective and impactful marketing campaigns that drive results.

Creating customer personas

Creating customer personas is an essential part of developing a successful marketing strategy. It involves identifying the traits and behaviors of your ideal customers and developing detailed profiles of them. This can help you understand your customers' needs, preferences, and pain points and tailor your marketing messages and tactics to meet them.

The first step in creating customer personas is to conduct research into your target audience. You need to gather data on customer demographics, buying patterns, and online behavior. This can involve conducting surveys or focus groups, or analyzing data from your website or social media platforms.

Once you have gathered enough data, you can identify common traits among your target audience, such as age, gender, income level, education, and job title. You can also consider psychographic factors such as personality, values, and lifestyle.

With this information, you can develop detailed profiles of your ideal customers, also known as customer personas. Each persona should have a name, a detailed description of their background and interests, and a list of their pain points, needs, and preferences.

It's important to prioritize your customer personas based on their importance to your business. This can help you focus your marketing efforts on the personas that are most likely to drive revenue and growth.

Once you have developed your customer personas, you can tailor your marketing messages and tactics to meet their specific needs and preferences. This can involve developing content that speaks directly to your personas' pain points, using language and imagery that resonates with them, and targeting your advertising and social media efforts to reach the right people.

It's important to continuously refine and update your customer personas based on new data and insights. As your business grows and evolves, so too will your target audience, and it's important to keep your personas up-to-date to ensure that your marketing efforts remain effective.

One of the biggest advantages of creating customer personas is that it helps you better understand your target audience. By having a detailed understanding of your ideal customers, you can develop marketing campaigns that are more likely to resonate with them.

Another advantage of creating customer personas is that it helps you tailor your marketing messages and tactics to meet the specific needs and preferences of your target audience. This can help you create more effective and impactful marketing campaigns that drive results.

In addition to tailoring your marketing messages and tactics, customer personas can also help you develop better products and services. By understanding your customers' needs and preferences, you can create products and services that are more likely to meet their needs and generate repeat business.

Another benefit of creating customer personas is that it can help you prioritize your marketing efforts. By focusing on the personas that are most likely to drive revenue and growth, you can optimize your marketing campaigns and generate more leads and sales.

Finally, customer personas can also help you save time and money on your marketing efforts. By targeting your marketing efforts to the right people, you can reduce wasteful spending on advertising and other marketing activities.

In summary, creating customer personas is a crucial step in developing a successful marketing strategy. It involves identifying the traits and behaviors of your ideal customers and developing detailed profiles of them. This can help you understand your customers' needs, preferences, and pain points and tailor your marketing messages and tactics to meet them. By focusing on the personas that are most likely to drive revenue and growth, you can optimize your marketing efforts and generate more leads and sales.

Conducting market research

Conducting market research is an essential step in developing a successful marketing strategy. It involves gathering information about your target audience, competitors, and market trends to gain insights into your industry and customer behavior. By conducting thorough market research, you can identify opportunities for growth, make informed decisions, and develop more effective marketing campaigns.

The process of conducting market research typically involves the following steps:

Identify your research objectives: The first step in conducting market research is to identify your research objectives. What do you want to learn? What are the key questions you need to answer? This will help you focus your research efforts and ensure that you are gathering the right information.

Determine your research methods: There are many different methods you can use to conduct market research, including surveys, focus groups, interviews, and online analytics. Each method has its own advantages and disadvantages, and the method you choose will depend on your research objectives and budget.

Develop your research questions: Once you have identified your research objectives and methods, you need to develop your research questions. What information do you need to gather to answer your key questions? Your research questions should be specific, measurable, and relevant to your research objectives.

Collect your data: Once you have developed your research questions, you can begin collecting your data. This can involve conducting surveys or focus groups, analyzing data from customer transactions and online behavior, or conducting interviews with industry experts.

Analyze your data: After collecting your data, you need to analyze it to gain insights into your target audience and market trends. This can involve organizing your data into charts and graphs, identifying trends and patterns, and developing insights and recommendations based on your findings.

Develop your marketing strategy: Finally, you can use the insights gained from your market research to develop your marketing strategy. This can involve tailoring your marketing messages and tactics to meet the needs and preferences of your target audience, identifying opportunities for growth and differentiation, and creating more effective marketing campaigns.

Identifying your research objectives: Before you start your market research, it's important to identify your research objectives. This involves clearly defining the questions you want to answer and the insights you want to gain. Your research objectives will guide your research efforts and help you stay focused on gathering the most relevant information.

Determining your research methods: There are many different methods you can use to conduct market research, and the method you choose will depend on your research objectives and budget. Surveys and focus groups are popular methods for gathering customer feedback, while analyzing data from online behavior and social media can provide insights into customer trends and preferences.

Developing your research questions: Once you have identified your research objectives and methods, you need to develop your research questions. These questions should be specific, measurable, and relevant to your research objectives. For example, if you're conducting a survey, your questions should be clear and easy to understand, and should elicit the information you need to answer your key questions.

Collecting your data: The next step is to collect your data. Depending on the method you choose, this can involve conducting surveys or focus groups, analyzing data from customer transactions or online behavior, or conducting interviews with industry experts. It's important to gather data from a representative sample of your target audience to ensure that your findings are accurate and reliable.

Analyzing your data: After collecting your data, you need to analyze it to gain insights into your target audience and market trends. This can involve organizing your data into charts and graphs, identifying trends and patterns, and developing insights and recommendations based on your findings. It's important to be objective in your analysis and to let the data speak for itself.

Developing your marketing strategy: Finally, you can use the insights gained from your market research to develop your marketing strategy. This involves tailoring your marketing messages and tactics to meet the needs and preferences of your target audience, identifying opportunities for growth and differentiation, and creating more effective marketing campaigns.

In summary, conducting market research is a critical step in developing a successful marketing strategy. By identifying your research objectives, determining your research methods, developing your research questions, collecting and analyzing your data, and using your findings to develop your marketing strategy, you can gain valuable insights into your target audience and market trends, and create more effective and impactful marketing campaigns.

Analyzing customer behavior

Analyzing customer behavior is a crucial aspect of developing an effective marketing strategy. It involves gathering and analyzing data on customer interactions with your brand, products, and services. By understanding customer behavior, you can gain valuable insights into their preferences, needs, and buying behavior. This, in turn, can help you develop more effective marketing campaigns, optimize your products and services, and improve the overall customer experience.

There are various methods for analyzing customer behavior, including web analytics, social media analytics, customer surveys, and sales data analysis. Web analytics tools, such as Google Analytics, can provide insights into customer behavior on your website, including metrics like page views, bounce rates, and time spent on site. Social media analytics tools can help you track customer engagement and behavior on social media platforms, including likes, shares, and comments. Customer surveys can provide direct feedback from customers on their experience with your brand, products, and services, as well as their preferences and needs. Finally, sales data analysis can help you understand customer buying behavior, including patterns, preferences, and trends.

By analyzing customer behavior, you can gain a deeper understanding of your customers and tailor your marketing efforts to meet their needs and preferences. For example, if you find that customers tend to abandon their shopping carts on your website, you can use that information to improve your checkout process and reduce cart abandonment. Similarly, if you find that customers are highly engaged with your brand on social media, you can use that information to develop more targeted and impactful social media campaigns.

In addition to improving your marketing campaigns and customer experience, analyzing customer behavior can also help you identify new opportunities for growth. For example, if you notice a particular segment of customers engaging with your brand more than others, you may want to focus your marketing efforts on that segment to attract more customers like them. Alternatively, if you identify a gap in the market based on customer behavior, you may want to develop new products or services to meet that need.

It's important to note that analyzing customer behavior is an ongoing process that requires continuous monitoring and refinement. Customer behavior is constantly changing, and you need to stay up-to-date with the latest trends and preferences to ensure that your marketing efforts remain effective. By continually analyzing customer behavior, you can stay ahead of the competition and adapt to changing market conditions.

Another benefit of analyzing customer behavior is that it can help you build stronger relationships with your customers. By understanding their needs and preferences, you can develop more personalized marketing messages and offer tailored products and services. This can help you build trust and loyalty with your customers, and increase the likelihood of repeat business and positive word-of-mouth referrals.

In summary, analyzing customer behavior is a critical component of developing a successful marketing strategy. By leveraging various methods to gather and analyze customer data, you can gain valuable insights into their preferences, needs, and buying behavior. This, in turn, can help you improve your marketing campaigns, optimize your products and services, identify new opportunities for growth, and build stronger relationships with your customers.

When analyzing customer behavior, it's important to keep in mind that customer behavior is influenced by many factors, including cultural, social, and psychological factors. For example, customers from different regions or cultures may have different preferences or buying behaviors. Similarly, customers may be influenced by their social networks, such as friends, family, or online communities. Understanding these factors can help you develop more effective marketing messages and strategies that resonate with your target audience.

In addition to understanding customer behavior, it's also important to analyze your competitors and industry trends. By keeping a pulse on your competitors' marketing strategies and products, you can identify areas where you can differentiate and stand out in the market. Similarly, by staying up-to-date on industry trends and changes, you can adjust your marketing strategies to remain relevant and competitive.

Ultimately, analyzing customer behavior is an ongoing process that requires a combination of data analysis, market research, and customer feedback. By continually gathering and analyzing customer data, you can stay ahead of the competition, improve your marketing campaigns, and deliver a better customer experience.

Chapter 3: Website development and optimization

Importance of website for small businesses

A website is a crucial tool for small businesses to establish an online presence and connect with potential customers. In today's digital age, having a website is not just a luxury but a necessity for small businesses looking to grow and succeed. A website serves as a virtual storefront, providing customers with a convenient and accessible way to learn about your business, products, and services.

A website is a 24/7 marketing tool that allows you to showcase your products and services to a global audience. It provides customers with a convenient way to learn about your business and make purchasing decisions. By having a website, you can reach customers beyond your local area and expand your customer base.

A website can help establish credibility and trust with potential customers. It's important to have a professional-looking website that reflects the values and personality of your business. Customers are more likely to trust and do business with companies that have a professional online presence.

A website can help you build stronger relationships with your customers. By providing valuable content and resources, you can engage with your customers and establish a sense of community around your brand. You can also use your website to collect customer feedback and respond to customer inquiries, which can help improve customer satisfaction and loyalty.

A website can provide valuable insights into customer behavior and preferences. By using web analytics tools, you can track customer behavior on your website, including page views, bounce rates, and time spent on site. This can help you optimize your website and marketing efforts to better meet the needs and preferences of your customers.

A website can help you compete with larger businesses in your industry. By establishing an online presence, you can level the playing field and compete on a global scale. A well-designed and optimized website can help you attract new customers, improve customer engagement and loyalty, and ultimately grow your business.

When it comes to designing a website for your small business, there are a few key elements to consider. Your website should be visually appealing and easy to navigate. A cluttered or confusing website can be a turn-off for potential customers and can lead to a high bounce rate.

Your website should be mobile-friendly and responsive. More and more people are accessing websites on their mobile devices, so it's important to ensure that your website is optimized for mobile viewing. This can improve the overall user experience and help keep customers engaged with your website.

Your website should have clear and concise messaging that conveys your brand values and value proposition. This can help customers understand what makes your business unique and why they should choose your products or services over those of your competitors.

Your website should have a clear call-to-action that encourages customers to take a desired action, whether that's making a purchase, filling out a contact form, or signing up for a newsletter. This can help improve conversion rates and drive more business for your company.

Your website should be optimized for search engines to ensure that potential customers can easily find your website when searching for relevant keywords. This can involve using strategic keywords in your website content and meta tags, optimizing your website structure and navigation, and building high-quality backlinks to your website.

In summary, having a website is a critical component of a small business's digital marketing strategy. It can help establish credibility and trust with customers, provide valuable insights into customer behavior and preferences, and help small businesses compete on a global scale. By designing a visually appealing, mobile-friendly, and optimized website with clear messaging and a strong call-to-action, small businesses can improve their online presence and drive more business.

Tips for website development and design

Developing and designing a website can be a challenging task, but it's essential for small businesses looking to establish an online presence and connect with potential customers. Here are some tips to help you develop and design a website that effectively showcases your products and services and engages your audience:

Define your goals and target audience: Before you start designing your website, it's important to define your goals and identify your target audience. What do you want to achieve with your website? Who is your target audience? By understanding your goals and target audience, you can tailor your website design and content to meet their needs and preferences.

Choose a user-friendly design: Your website design should be visually appealing, easy to navigate, and user-friendly. This includes choosing a clear and readable font, using a consistent color scheme, and ensuring that your website is easy to navigate. A user-friendly design can improve the overall user experience and help keep customers engaged with your website.

Optimize for mobile devices: More and more people are accessing websites on their mobile devices, so it's important to ensure that your website is optimized for mobile viewing. This can involve using responsive design, which automatically adjusts your website layout to fit different screen sizes, and optimizing your website loading speed for mobile devices.

Use high-quality images and videos: Visual content, such as images and videos, can help engage your audience and showcase your products and services. It's important to use high-quality images and videos that accurately represent your brand and products.

Ensure website security: Website security is crucial for protecting your business and customer data. This includes using secure hosting and encryption, regularly updating software and plugins, and using strong passwords and authentication.

Optimize for search engines: Search engine optimization (SEO) is essential for improving your website's visibility and attracting more potential customers. This involves using strategic keywords in your website content and meta tags, optimizing your website structure and navigation, and building high-quality backlinks to your website.

Test and optimize: Finally, it's important to regularly test and optimize your website to ensure that it's effective in achieving your goals and meeting the needs of your target audience. This can involve analyzing website traffic data, conducting user testing, and making regular updates to your website content and design.

Branding: Your website should accurately reflect your brand identity, including your brand values, personality, and style. This can involve using consistent branding elements such as your logo, color scheme, and messaging throughout your website.

Content strategy: Your website content should be strategic, informative, and engaging. This can involve using a mix of written content, images, videos, and other multimedia to showcase your products and services and provide value to your audience.

Website functionality: Your website should be functional and easy to use, with features such as a search function, contact forms, and clear navigation. This can help improve the overall user experience and make it easier for customers to engage with your business.

Social media integration: Social media can be a powerful tool for promoting your business and engaging with customers. Your website should include social media integration, allowing customers to easily follow and engage with your brand on social media platforms.

Analytics and tracking: It's important to regularly track website analytics and use that data to make informed decisions about your website design and content. This can involve using tools such as Google Analytics to track website traffic, bounce rates, and other metrics.

When it comes to website development and design, it's important to remember that the process is ongoing. Your website should be a dynamic tool that is regularly updated and optimized to reflect changes in your business, industry trends, and customer needs and preferences. This can involve making regular updates to your website content, adding new features and functionality, and staying up-to-date with the latest web design trends and best practices.

It's also important to ensure that your website is accessible to all users, including those with disabilities. This can involve using alt text for images, providing captions for videos, and using website design that is optimized for screen readers and other assistive technologies.

Finally, it's important to work with a reputable web development team that has the expertise and experience to create a website that effectively represents your brand and meets the needs of your target audience. This can involve working with a web development agency, hiring a freelance web developer, or using website builder tools that provide customizable templates and drag-and-drop design features.

In conclusion, website development and design is a critical component of a small business's digital marketing strategy. By following best practices such as defining your goals and target audience, choosing a user-friendly design, optimizing for mobile devices and search engines, and regularly testing and optimizing your website, you can create a website that effectively showcases your products and services and engages your audience. By working with a reputable web development team and staying up-to-date with the latest web design trends and best practices, you can create a website that helps your business succeed online.

Search engine optimization (SEO) strategies

Search engine optimization (SEO) is an essential component of any successful digital marketing strategy for small businesses. By optimizing your website and content for search engines, you can improve your website's visibility and attract more potential customers to your website. There are several effective SEO strategies that small businesses can implement to improve their search engine rankings and drive more traffic to their website.

One of the first steps in developing an effective SEO strategy is conducting keyword research. Keyword research involves identifying the search terms that potential customers are using to find businesses like yours. By using these keywords strategically in your website content, meta tags, and other areas, you can improve your website's visibility in search engine results pages.

Another important aspect of SEO is optimizing your website structure and navigation. Your website should be easy to understand and navigate for both users and search engines. This can involve using a clear hierarchy of content, organizing your content into categories, and using descriptive URLs.

Optimizing your website content is also crucial for SEO success. Your website content should be optimized for search engines and provide value to your audience. This can involve using strategic keywords in your content, using header tags to organize your content, and regularly updating your website with fresh, high-quality content.

Building high-quality backlinks is another effective SEO strategy for small businesses. Backlinks are links from other websites to your website. By building high-quality backlinks from reputable websites, you can improve your website's authority and visibility in search engine results pages.

Optimizing your website for local search is also important for small businesses with a local presence. This can involve using location-specific keywords in your website content, creating local business listings on directories like Google My Business, and getting reviews from customers in your local area.

Social media can also be a powerful tool for improving your website's visibility and attracting more potential customers. By sharing your website content on social media platforms and engaging with your audience, you can improve your website's authority and drive more traffic to your website.

Regularly monitoring and analyzing your website performance is crucial for identifying areas for improvement and making adjustments to your SEO strategy. This can involve using tools like Google Analytics to track website traffic and other metrics, and making adjustments to your SEO strategy based on the data.

It's important to note that SEO is not a one-time task but an ongoing process. Search engine algorithms and user behavior are constantly evolving, so it's essential to regularly review and adjust your SEO strategy to ensure that it remains effective. This means staying up-to-date with the latest SEO trends and best practices, monitoring your website's performance and making adjustments as needed, and continuously testing and optimizing your website to improve its search engine rankings.

It's also important to remember that SEO is just one aspect of your overall digital marketing strategy. While SEO can be highly effective in driving organic traffic to your website, it's important to also consider other digital marketing tactics such as social media marketing, paid advertising, email marketing, and content marketing.

Also, an effective digital marketing strategy for small businesses should involve a holistic approach that incorporates multiple tactics and channels. By combining SEO with other digital marketing tactics, small businesses can create a comprehensive and effective strategy that helps them reach their target audience, improve their online visibility, and drive more business.

In addition to the strategies discussed, there are also several best practices that small businesses should follow when it comes to SEO:

Avoid "black hat" SEO tactics: These are tactics that attempt to manipulate search engine rankings by using unethical techniques such as keyword stuffing, hidden text, and cloaking. Not only can these tactics be ineffective, but they can also lead to your website being penalized or even banned from search engines.

Use descriptive and relevant meta tags: Meta tags, including title tags and meta descriptions, are important for helping search engines understand what your website is about. Use relevant keywords in your meta tags and make sure they accurately reflect the content on your website.

Use header tags: Header tags (H1, H2, H3) can help break up your content and make it easier to read for both users and search engines. Use relevant keywords in your header tags to help improve your website's search engine rankings.

Use alt tags for images: Alt tags provide a text description of images on your website, making them accessible to users who use assistive technologies like screen readers. Use descriptive alt tags that accurately describe the image and include relevant keywords.

Monitor website loading speed: Website loading speed is an important factor in both user experience and search engine rankings. Use tools like Google PageSpeed Insights to monitor your website's loading speed and make adjustments as needed.

By following these best practices and implementing effective SEO strategies, small businesses can improve their online visibility, attract more potential customers, and ultimately drive more business. However, it's important to remember that SEO is a long-term process that requires consistent effort and attention to be effective. By staying up-to-date with the latest trends and best practices and continuously testing and optimizing your website, you can create an SEO strategy that helps your small business succeed online.

Mobile optimization and responsiveness

Mobile optimization and responsiveness is a critical aspect of website design for small businesses. With more and more users accessing websites on mobile devices, having a website that is optimized for mobile devices is essential for providing a good user experience and improving your search engine rankings.

Mobile optimization involves designing your website to be easily viewable and functional on mobile devices such as smartphones and tablets. This can involve using responsive design, which is a design approach that ensures your website content adapts to the size of the screen it's being viewed on.

Having a responsive website is important for several reasons. First, it provides a better user experience for mobile users, as they can easily view and interact with your website without having to zoom in or scroll horizontally. Second, it can improve your website's search engine rankings. In 2015, Google announced that it would be using mobile-friendliness as a ranking factor in search results. This means that websites that are not mobile-friendly may not appear as high in search results as websites that are mobile-friendly.

When designing your website for mobile devices, there are several factors to consider. These include:

Navigation: Your website navigation should be clear and easy to use on mobile devices. This can involve using a mobile-friendly navigation menu, using clear labels for buttons and links, and minimizing the number of clicks required to access important content.

Layout: Your website layout should be optimized for mobile devices, with content that is easily readable and accessible on smaller screens. This can involve using a responsive design approach, using larger font sizes, and avoiding content that is too wide for smaller screens.

Load times: Mobile users expect websites to load quickly on their devices. This means optimizing your website's load times by using compressed images, minimizing the use of scripts, and leveraging browser caching.

Forms: If your website includes forms for users to fill out, make sure they are optimized for mobile devices. This can involve using a mobile-friendly form layout, minimizing the number of form fields, and using input types that are optimized for mobile devices.

By optimizing your website for mobile devices, you can improve your website's user experience, increase your website's search engine rankings, and ultimately drive more business. With more and more users accessing websites on mobile devices, having a mobile-friendly website is no longer an option, but a necessity for small businesses looking to succeed online.

In addition to the factors mentioned earlier, there are some other aspects that small businesses should consider when optimizing their website for mobile devices. These include:

Button and link sizes: Buttons and links on your website should be large enough and spaced far enough apart to make them easy to tap on a touchscreen device.

Visual content: Visual content, including images and videos, should be optimized for mobile devices. This can involve using compressed images, using responsive video players, and avoiding content that requires Adobe Flash, which is not supported on many mobile devices.

Mobile-friendly features: There are several features that can improve your website's mobile-friendliness, including click-to-call buttons, maps and directions, and social media sharing buttons.

Test and optimize: It's important to regularly test your website on mobile devices to ensure that it is functioning properly and providing a good user experience. You can use tools like Google's Mobile-Friendly Test to check your website's mobile-friendliness and identify areas for improvement.

It's important to remember that optimizing your website for mobile devices is not a one-time task, but an ongoing process. As new mobile devices and technologies are introduced, it's important to continually update and optimize your website to ensure that it remains accessible and functional on all devices.

In conclusion, mobile optimization and responsiveness is a critical aspect of website design for small businesses. By optimizing your website for mobile devices, you can improve your website's user experience, increase your website's search engine rankings, and ultimately drive more business. By considering factors like navigation, layout, load times, forms, button and link sizes, visual content, mobile-friendly features, and regularly testing and optimizing your website, small businesses can create a mobile-friendly website that helps them succeed online.

Chapter 4: Social media marketing

Role of social media in digital marketing

Social media has become a crucial component of digital marketing for small businesses. Social media platforms like Facebook, Twitter, Instagram, and LinkedIn offer small businesses a powerful tool for connecting with their target audience, building their brand, and driving traffic to their website.

One of the primary benefits of social media for small businesses is its ability to provide a platform for engaging with customers and building relationships. By posting content that is relevant and interesting to your audience, responding to customer inquiries and feedback, and sharing user-generated content, you can build a loyal following on social media and establish your brand as an authority in your industry.

Social media also offers small businesses a cost-effective way to promote their products and services. By using targeted advertising on social media platforms, small businesses can reach potential customers who are likely to be interested in their products or services. This can involve using audience targeting tools to identify users based on factors like age, location, interests, and behaviors, and creating ads that are specifically designed to appeal to these users.

In addition to advertising, social media also provides a valuable platform for content marketing. By creating and sharing high-quality content on social media platforms, small businesses can establish themselves as thought leaders in their industry and build a loyal following of engaged users. This can involve creating blog posts, videos, infographics, and other types of content that provide value to your audience and demonstrate your expertise in your field.

Another benefit of social media for small businesses is its ability to drive traffic to your website. By including links to your website in your social media posts and profiles, you can direct users to your website and encourage them to learn more about your products and services. This can be particularly effective when combined with targeted advertising, as you can direct users to specific pages on your website that are designed to convert them into customers.

It's important to note that social media should not be viewed as a standalone marketing strategy, but rather as one aspect of a comprehensive digital marketing plan. Social media should be integrated with other digital marketing tactics, including search engine optimization, content marketing, email marketing, and paid advertising, to create a holistic approach that maximizes your reach and effectiveness.

When developing a social media strategy for your small business, there are several best practices to keep in mind:

Choose the right platforms: Not all social media platforms are created equal. Choose the platforms that are most relevant to your target audience and the ones where your brand is most likely to succeed. For example, if you are targeting young consumers, Instagram may be a more effective platform than LinkedIn.

Create a content strategy: Develop a content strategy that is aligned with your business goals and target audience. Create content that is relevant, engaging, and valuable to your audience, and post it consistently to keep your followers engaged.

Engage with your audience: Social media is all about two-way communication. Respond to comments and messages promptly, and actively engage with your followers by asking questions, soliciting feedback, and encouraging user-generated content.

Measure your results: Use analytics tools to track your social media performance and measure the impact of your social media efforts on your business goals. Adjust your strategy based on what is working and what is not working.

Stay up-to-date with trends: Social media is constantly evolving, so it's important to stay up-to-date with the latest trends and best practices. Attend industry events, read industry blogs, and follow thought leaders on social media to stay ahead of the curve.

In conclusion, social media plays a critical role in digital marketing for small businesses. By providing a platform for engaging with customers, promoting products and services, content marketing, and driving website traffic, social media can help small businesses reach their target audience, build their brand, and ultimately drive more business. By developing a strong social media strategy that is aligned with your business goals and target audience, small businesses can leverage the power of social media to succeed online.

Popular social media platforms for small businesses

There are several social media platforms that are particularly well-suited for small businesses. Each platform has its own unique features and benefits, and the best platform for your business will depend on your target audience, business goals, and the types of content you want to create.

Here are some of the most popular social media platforms for small businesses:

Facebook: With over 2 billion active users, Facebook is one of the most popular social media platforms for small businesses. Facebook provides a powerful tool for engaging with customers, promoting products and services, and building brand awareness. Small businesses can use Facebook to create a business page, share content, run targeted ads, and interact with customers through comments, messages, and reviews.

Instagram: Instagram is a visual platform that is particularly well-suited for businesses that have a strong visual component, such as fashion, beauty, and food. With over 1 billion active users, Instagram provides a powerful tool for building brand awareness and engaging with customers through visually stunning content. Small businesses can use Instagram to create a business profile, share photos and videos, use hashtags to reach new audiences, and run targeted ads.

Twitter: Twitter is a platform that is particularly well-suited for businesses that want to engage with customers in real-time and share updates on current events or industry news. With over 330 million active users, Twitter provides a powerful tool for building brand awareness and engaging with customers through short, timely updates. Small businesses can use Twitter to create a business profile, share updates, participate in conversations, and run targeted ads.

LinkedIn: LinkedIn is a platform that is particularly well-suited for businesses that are targeting other businesses or professionals. With over 700 million active users, LinkedIn provides a powerful tool for building professional networks, promoting products and services, and sharing industry news and updates. Small businesses can use LinkedIn to create a business page, share updates, participate in groups, and run targeted ads.

YouTube: YouTube is a platform that is particularly well-suited for businesses that want to create and share video content. With over 2 billion active users, YouTube provides a powerful tool for building brand awareness and engaging with customers through video content. Small businesses can use YouTube to create a channel, share video content, optimize videos for search, and run targeted ads.

In conclusion, there are several social media platforms that are particularly well-suited for small businesses. Each platform has its own unique features and benefits, and the best platform for your business will depend on your target audience, business goals, and the types of content you want to create. By selecting the right social media platform(s) for your business and creating a strong social media strategy, small businesses can leverage the power of social media to reach their target audience, build their brand, and ultimately drive more business.

It's important to note that while these social media platforms can be powerful tools for small businesses, it's important to use them strategically and effectively. Here are some best practices for using social media effectively as a small business:

Know your audience: Understanding your target audience is critical for creating effective social media content. Know who your customers are, what they care about, and what motivates them to engage with your brand.

Create engaging content: Social media is all about creating content that resonates with your audience. Use high-quality images, videos, and other types of content that are relevant and interesting to your audience.

Use hashtags: Hashtags are a powerful tool for reaching new audiences and increasing engagement on social media. Use relevant hashtags that are popular among your target audience, and include them in your social media posts.

Engage with your followers: Social media is a two-way conversation. Respond to comments and messages promptly, and actively engage with your followers by asking questions, soliciting feedback, and encouraging user-generated content.

Track your performance: Use analytics tools to track your social media performance and measure the impact of your social media efforts on your business goals. Adjust your strategy based on what is working and what is not working.

75

By following these best practices, small businesses can use social media to reach their target audience, build their brand, and ultimately drive more business. It's important to remember that social media is just one aspect of a comprehensive digital marketing plan, and that it should be used in conjunction with other digital marketing tactics to create a holistic approach that maximizes your reach and effectiveness.

Content creation and management

Content creation and management is a critical aspect of digital marketing for small businesses. In order to effectively reach your target audience and build your brand, you need to create high-quality, relevant, and engaging content that resonates with your audience. This can involve creating a wide range of content types, including blog posts, videos, infographics, social media posts, and more.

One of the first steps in content creation and management is defining your content strategy. This involves understanding your target audience, identifying their needs and interests, and creating content that addresses those needs and interests. You should also consider the type of content you want to create, the channels you want to use to distribute your content, and how you will measure the success of your content.

Once you have a content strategy in place, the next step is to create your content. This can involve writing blog posts, creating videos, designing infographics, and more. It's important to ensure that your content is high-quality, relevant, and engaging, and that it aligns with your brand's messaging and tone.

After you have created your content, the next step is to manage and distribute it. This can involve using a content management system (CMS) to organize your content, schedule your content for publication, and track your content's performance. You can also use social media and other channels to distribute your content to your target audience.

In addition to creating and managing your content, it's important to continually measure and optimize your content performance. This can involve using analytics tools to track your content's performance, analyzing the results to identify areas for improvement, and adjusting your content strategy and creation approach accordingly.

Some best practices for content creation and management for small businesses include:

- Understand your target audience and their needs.
- Create high-quality, relevant, and engaging content.
- Use a content management system (CMS) to organize and schedule your content.
- Distribute your content across multiple channels, including social media.

- Measure your content's performance and adjust your strategy accordingly.

It's important to note that content creation and management is an ongoing process, and it requires a significant investment of time, resources, and expertise. For many small businesses, it can be challenging to create high-quality content consistently, which is why outsourcing content creation to a professional agency or freelancer can be a smart investment.

In addition to outsourcing content creation, small businesses can also leverage user-generated content (UGC) as a cost-effective way to create engaging content. UGC involves encouraging your customers to create and share content related to your brand, such as photos, videos, or reviews. By showcasing UGC on your website and social media channels, you can build brand loyalty and create a sense of community around your brand.

Another important aspect of content creation and management is search engine optimization (SEO). SEO involves optimizing your content and website to improve your visibility on search engine results pages (SERPs). By incorporating relevant keywords, meta descriptions, and other SEO best practices into your content, you can increase your chances of appearing higher on SERPs and attracting more organic traffic to your website.

Finally, it's important to ensure that your content is accessible and optimized for mobile devices. With more and more consumers accessing the internet through mobile devices, it's essential that your content is mobile-friendly and easy to read and navigate on small screens.

In conclusion, content creation and management is a critical aspect of digital marketing for small businesses. By creating high-quality, relevant, and engaging content that resonates with your audience, and managing and distributing that content effectively, small businesses can build their brand, reach their target audience, and ultimately drive more business. By following best practices like understanding your target audience, using a content management system, and measuring your content's performance, small businesses can create a content strategy that helps them succeed online.

Additionally, it's important to consider the different stages of the buyer's journey when creating and managing your content. The buyer's journey consists of three stages: awareness, consideration, and decision. At each stage, your target audience has different needs and interests, and your content should be tailored accordingly.

During the awareness stage, your target audience is just becoming aware of their problem or need, and they are looking for information to help them better understand the issue. At this stage, your content should be educational and informative, and it should help your target audience understand the problem or need they are facing.

During the consideration stage, your target audience has identified their problem or need, and they are actively looking for solutions. At this stage, your content should focus on showcasing the benefits of your product or service, and it should help your target audience evaluate their options and make an informed decision.

During the decision stage, your target audience has narrowed down their options and is ready to make a purchase decision. At this stage, your content should focus on helping your target audience make the final decision to purchase your product or service, and it should provide them with the information and reassurance they need to feel confident in their decision.

By tailoring your content to the different stages of the buyer's journey, you can create a more effective content strategy that helps you reach your target audience at the right time with the right message.

In conclusion, content creation and management is a critical aspect of digital marketing for small businesses. By creating high-quality, relevant, and engaging content that resonates with your audience, and managing and distributing that content effectively, small businesses can build their brand, reach their target audience, and ultimately drive more business. By following best practices like understanding your target audience, using a content management system, measuring your content's performance, and tailoring your content to the different stages of the buyer's journey, small businesses can create a content strategy that helps them succeed online.

Social media advertising and promotion

Social media advertising and promotion is a powerful tool for small businesses looking to reach their target audience and drive more business. With social media advertising, small businesses can create highly targeted ads that reach the right audience at the right time, and with social media promotion, they can boost the visibility of their organic posts to reach a wider audience.

One of the biggest benefits of social media advertising and promotion is the ability to target your ads to specific demographics, interests, and behaviors. This allows you to create highly personalized and relevant ads that are more likely to resonate with your target audience and drive engagement.

There are several types of social media ads that small businesses can use, including:

Sponsored content: These are ads that appear in a user's social media feed, and they look similar to regular posts. Sponsored content can include text, images, videos, and other types of content.

Display ads: These are ads that appear on the sides or top of a user's social media feed. They can include images, text, and other types of content.

Video ads: These are ads that appear as videos in a user's social media feed. Video ads can be highly engaging and effective at capturing a user's attention.

Sponsored stories: These are ads that appear as a user's story in a social media platform, and they are only available on certain platforms like Instagram and Facebook.

In addition to social media advertising, small businesses can also use social media promotion to boost the visibility of their organic posts. Social media promotion involves paying to boost the visibility of a post to reach a wider audience. This can be a cost-effective way to increase engagement on your organic posts and reach a wider audience.

Some best practices for social media advertising and promotion for small businesses include:

- Target your ads to specific demographics, interests, and behaviors.
- Use eye-catching visuals and compelling messaging to capture your audience's attention.
- Test different ad formats and messaging to find what works best for your audience.
- Use analytics tools to measure the effectiveness of your ads and adjust your strategy accordingly.
- Set a clear budget and goals for your social media advertising and promotion efforts.

It's important to note that social media advertising and promotion can be complex and time-consuming, and it requires a certain level of expertise to be successful. For many small businesses, outsourcing social media advertising and promotion to a professional agency or freelancer can be a smart investment.

In addition to outsourcing, small businesses can also leverage social media influencers to promote their brand and products. Social media influencers are individuals who have a large following on social media and can help promote your brand to their audience. By partnering with social media influencers who have a similar target audience, small businesses can increase their reach and credibility on social media.

Another important aspect of social media advertising and promotion is measuring and analyzing your results. Using analytics tools, you can track the performance of your ads and promotion efforts, and adjust your strategy accordingly. By analyzing your results, you can identify which ads and campaigns are most effective, and adjust your budget and targeting to maximize your return on investment.

Finally, it's important to ensure that your social media advertising and promotion efforts are integrated with your overall digital marketing strategy. Social media advertising and promotion should be used in conjunction with other digital marketing tactics, such as email marketing, content creation, and SEO, to create a comprehensive approach that maximizes your reach and effectiveness.

In conclusion, social media advertising and promotion is a powerful tool for small businesses looking to reach their target audience and drive more business. By creating highly targeted and personalized ads, and boosting the visibility of organic posts, small businesses can increase engagement, build their brand, and ultimately drive more business. By following best practices like targeting your ads, using compelling visuals and messaging, testing different ad formats, and measuring your results, small businesses can create a social media advertising and promotion strategy that helps them succeed online. By integrating social media advertising and promotion with other digital marketing tactics, small businesses can create a holistic approach that maximizes their reach and effectiveness online.

Chapter 5: Email marketing

The importance of email marketing for small businesses

Email marketing is a powerful tool for small businesses looking to reach their target audience and drive more business. With email marketing, small businesses can create personalized and targeted messages that are more likely to resonate with their audience and drive engagement.

One of the biggest benefits of email marketing is its cost-effectiveness. Unlike traditional advertising methods, email marketing is relatively inexpensive, and it can be a great way for small businesses with limited budgets to reach their target audience.

Another important benefit of email marketing is its ability to provide measurable results. By using analytics tools, small businesses can track the effectiveness of their email campaigns, and adjust their strategy accordingly. This allows them to continually improve their email marketing efforts and maximize their return on investment.

In addition to being cost-effective and measurable, email marketing is also highly customizable. Small businesses can create personalized messages that are tailored to specific segments of their audience, based on factors like demographics, interests, and purchase history. This can help increase engagement and build brand loyalty among their target audience.

Some best practices for email marketing for small businesses include:

Building a targeted email list: Small businesses should focus on building an email list of individuals who are interested in their products or services, and who have given permission to receive emails from them.

Creating personalized messages: Small businesses should create personalized messages that speak to their audience's needs and interests, and that are tailored to specific segments of their audience.

Using a clear and compelling subject line: The subject line is the first thing that the recipient sees, so it's important to make it clear and compelling in order to increase the chances that the email will be opened.

Including a clear call-to-action (CTA): Every email should include a clear and compelling call-to-action that encourages the recipient to take action, such as making a purchase, signing up for a newsletter, or following the business on social media.

Using analytics tools to measure results: Small businesses should use analytics tools to track the effectiveness of their email campaigns, and adjust their strategy accordingly.

It's important to note that email marketing is not a one-time effort, but rather an ongoing process that requires a significant investment of time, resources, and expertise. For many small businesses, outsourcing email marketing to a professional agency or freelancer can be a smart investment.

In addition to outsourcing, small businesses can also leverage marketing automation tools to streamline their email marketing efforts. Marketing automation involves using software to automate certain tasks, such as sending targeted emails based on specific triggers, like a new subscriber or a recent purchase. This can help small businesses save time and resources while still delivering personalized and targeted messages to their audience.

Another important aspect of email marketing is compliance with anti-spam laws. Small businesses should be aware of and comply with anti-spam laws, which regulate how businesses can send commercial email messages. This includes things like providing a clear opt-out mechanism for recipients, and including a physical mailing address in the email message.

Finally, it's important to ensure that your email marketing efforts are integrated with your overall digital marketing strategy. Email marketing should be used in conjunction with other digital marketing tactics, such as social media advertising, content creation, and SEO, to create a comprehensive approach that maximizes your reach and effectiveness.

In conclusion, email marketing is a powerful tool for small businesses looking to reach their target audience and drive more business. By creating personalized and targeted messages, small businesses can increase engagement and build brand loyalty among their audience. By following best practices like building a targeted email list, creating personalized messages, using a clear and compelling subject line, including a clear call-to-action, using analytics tools to measure results, and complying with anti-spam laws, small businesses can create an effective email marketing strategy that helps them succeed online. By integrating email marketing with other digital marketing tactics, small businesses can create a holistic approach that maximizes their reach and effectiveness online.

Building an email list

Building an email list is a critical component of email marketing for small businesses. An email list is a collection of email addresses that have been voluntarily provided by individuals who are interested in receiving emails from your business. By building a targeted email list, small businesses can reach their audience directly and deliver personalized and targeted messages that drive engagement and sales.

One of the most important things to keep in mind when building an email list is to focus on quality over quantity. It's important to build a list of individuals who are genuinely interested in your products or services and who have given permission to receive emails from your business. This can help ensure that your emails are more likely to be opened, read, and engaged with, and can help you build a loyal customer base over time.

There are several strategies that small businesses can use to build their email list, including:

Offering incentives: Small businesses can offer incentives like discounts, freebies, or exclusive content to encourage individuals to sign up for their email list.

Using lead magnets: Lead magnets are valuable resources, like ebooks, whitepapers, or webinars, that individuals can access in exchange for their email address.

Optimizing website forms: Small businesses can optimize their website forms to make it easy for individuals to sign up for their email list, such as by placing the form prominently on the homepage or offering a pop-up form.

Using social media: Small businesses can promote their email list on social media platforms, such as by offering a sign-up form on their Facebook page or promoting their lead magnet on Instagram.

Offering a referral program: Small businesses can offer a referral program that rewards individuals for referring their friends and family to sign up for their email list.

It's also important to regularly clean and maintain your email list to ensure that it remains effective over time. This includes removing inactive or invalid email addresses and segmenting your list based on factors like engagement or purchase history.

It's important to note that building an email list is an ongoing process that requires a significant investment of time, resources, and expertise. For many small businesses, outsourcing email list building to a professional agency or freelancer can be a smart investment.

In addition to outsourcing, small businesses can also leverage marketing automation tools to streamline their email list building efforts. Marketing automation involves using software to automate certain tasks, such as sending targeted emails based on specific triggers, like a new subscriber or a recent purchase. This can help small businesses save time and resources while still building a high-quality email list.

Another important aspect of building an email list is compliance with anti-spam laws. Small businesses should be aware of and comply with anti-spam laws, which regulate how businesses can collect and use email addresses. This includes things like providing a clear opt-in mechanism for individuals to sign up for your email list, and including a physical mailing address in your email messages.

Finally, it's important to ensure that your email list building efforts are integrated with your overall digital marketing strategy. Building an email list should be used in conjunction with other digital marketing tactics, such as social media advertising, content creation, and SEO, to create a comprehensive approach that maximizes your reach and effectiveness.

In conclusion, building an email list is a critical component of email marketing for small businesses. By focusing on quality over quantity and using strategies like offering incentives, using lead magnets, optimizing website forms, using social media, and offering a referral program, small businesses can build a targeted email list that drives engagement and sales. By following best practices like regularly cleaning and maintaining your email list, complying with anti-spam laws, and integrating email list building with other digital marketing tactics, small businesses can create an effective email list building strategy that helps them succeed online.

Creating effective email campaigns

Creating effective email campaigns is essential for small businesses looking to reach their target audience and drive more business. An effective email campaign should be personalized, targeted, and engaging, and should encourage the recipient to take action, such as making a purchase, signing up for a newsletter, or following the business on social media.

Some best practices for creating effective email campaigns include:

Personalizing the message: Personalization is key to creating an effective email campaign. Small businesses should use the recipient's name, and tailor the message to their interests and preferences.

Creating a clear and compelling subject line: The subject line is the first thing that the recipient sees, so it's important to make it clear and compelling in order to increase the chances that the email will be opened.

Using a clear call-to-action (CTA): Every email should include a clear and compelling call-to-action that encourages the recipient to take action, such as making a purchase, signing up for a newsletter, or following the business on social media.

Segmenting the email list: Small businesses should segment their email list based on factors like engagement or purchase history, and create targeted messages that are tailored to specific segments of their audience.

Using engaging visuals: Visuals can help increase engagement and make your email stand out. Small businesses should use engaging visuals like images or videos to help convey their message.

Testing different elements: Small businesses should test different elements of their email campaigns, such as subject lines, CTAs, and visuals, to see what works best for their audience.

Analyzing results: Small businesses should use analytics tools to track the effectiveness of their email campaigns, and adjust their strategy accordingly.

It's also important to ensure that your email campaigns are integrated with your overall digital marketing strategy. Email campaigns should be used in conjunction with other digital marketing tactics, such as social media advertising, content creation, and SEO, to create a comprehensive approach that maximizes your reach and effectiveness.

It's important to note that creating effective email campaigns is not a one-time effort, but rather an ongoing process that requires a significant investment of time, resources, and expertise. For many small businesses, outsourcing email campaign creation to a professional agency or freelancer can be a smart investment.

In addition to outsourcing, small businesses can also leverage marketing automation tools to streamline their email campaign creation efforts. Marketing automation involves using software to automate certain tasks, such as sending targeted emails based on specific triggers, like a new subscriber or a recent purchase. This can help small businesses save time and resources while still delivering personalized and targeted messages to their audience.

Another important aspect of creating effective email campaigns is compliance with anti-spam laws. Small businesses should be aware of and comply with anti-spam laws, which regulate how businesses can send commercial email messages. This includes things like providing a clear opt-out mechanism for recipients, and including a physical mailing address in the email message.

Finally, it's important to ensure that your email campaigns are integrated with your overall digital marketing strategy. Email campaigns should be used in conjunction with other digital marketing tactics, such as social media advertising, content creation, and SEO, to create a comprehensive approach that maximizes your reach and effectiveness.

In conclusion, creating effective email campaigns is essential for small businesses looking to reach their target audience and drive more business. By personalizing the message, creating a clear and compelling subject line, using a clear call-to-action, segmenting the email list, using engaging visuals, testing different elements, and analyzing results, small businesses can create an effective email campaign that resonates with their audience. By outsourcing, leveraging marketing automation, complying with anti-spam laws, and integrating email campaigns with other digital marketing tactics, small businesses can create an effective and efficient email campaign strategy that helps them succeed online.

Measuring email marketing success

Measuring email marketing success is critical for small businesses looking to understand the effectiveness of their email campaigns and make data-driven decisions. By using analytics tools to track metrics like open rates, click-through rates, and conversion rates, small businesses can gain valuable insights into how their email campaigns are performing and adjust their strategy accordingly.

Some key metrics that small businesses should track when measuring email marketing success include:

Open rate: The open rate is the percentage of recipients who opened the email. This metric can help businesses understand how well their subject line is performing, and how engaged their audience is.

Click-through rate (CTR): The click-through rate is the percentage of recipients who clicked on a link within the email. This metric can help businesses understand how well their message is resonating with their audience, and how effective their call-to-action is.

Conversion rate: The conversion rate is the percentage of recipients who took a desired action after clicking through the email, such as making a purchase or signing up for a newsletter. This metric can help businesses understand how well their email campaigns are driving business results.

Bounce rate: The bounce rate is the percentage of emails that were not delivered to the recipient. This can happen if the email address is invalid or if the recipient's inbox is full. A high bounce rate can indicate issues with email list quality or targeting.

Unsubscribe rate: The unsubscribe rate is the percentage of recipients who opted out of receiving future emails. A high unsubscribe rate can indicate issues with email frequency, relevance, or targeting.

Small businesses should also segment their email list and track metrics for each segment separately, as different segments may respond differently to different types of emails.

In addition to tracking metrics, small businesses should use the data to make data-driven decisions and adjust their email marketing strategy accordingly. This may include changing the subject line, adjusting the frequency of emails, segmenting the list differently, or creating different types of content.

It's important to note that measuring email marketing success is an ongoing process that requires regular monitoring and adjustment. By tracking key metrics, segmenting the email list, and making data-driven decisions, small businesses can create an effective email marketing strategy that helps them reach their audience and drive more business.

In addition to tracking metrics, small businesses can use A/B testing to experiment with different elements of their email campaigns and determine which ones are most effective. A/B testing involves creating two versions of an email, each with a different variable (such as subject line, call-to-action, or visual element), and sending them to different segments of the email list. By comparing the results of the two versions, small businesses can determine which variable is more effective and adjust their strategy accordingly.

Another important aspect of measuring email marketing success is understanding the customer journey. Small businesses should use analytics tools to track the entire customer journey, from the initial email open to the final purchase or conversion. This can help businesses understand how their email campaigns are impacting the overall customer experience and identify areas for improvement.

Finally, it's important to ensure that your email marketing efforts are integrated with your overall digital marketing strategy. Email marketing should be used in conjunction with other digital marketing tactics, such as social media advertising, content creation, and SEO, to create a comprehensive approach that maximizes your reach and effectiveness.

By measuring email marketing success, small businesses can gain a deeper understanding of their audience and improve their email campaigns over time. By continuously analyzing metrics and making data-driven decisions, small businesses can optimize their email campaigns for maximum impact and effectiveness.

In addition to analyzing metrics and making data-driven decisions, small businesses should also prioritize building relationships with their email subscribers. This can involve sending personalized messages, offering exclusive promotions or discounts, and creating valuable content that resonates with their audience.

Ultimately, the key to success with email marketing is understanding your audience and providing them with relevant, engaging content that encourages them to take action. By following best practices for email campaign creation, measuring success with analytics tools, using A/B testing to experiment with different variables, understanding the customer journey, and building relationships with subscribers, small businesses can create an effective and efficient email marketing strategy that helps them succeed online.

In conclusion, measuring email marketing success is critical for small businesses looking to understand the effectiveness of their email campaigns and make data-driven decisions. By tracking metrics like open rate, click-through rate, conversion rate, bounce rate, and unsubscribe rate, small businesses can gain valuable insights into how their email campaigns are performing and adjust their strategy accordingly. By segmenting the email list, using analytics tools, and making data-driven decisions, small businesses can create an effective email marketing strategy that helps them succeed online.

Chapter 6: Pay-per-click (PPC) advertising

Definition of PPC advertising

PPC advertising, or pay-per-click advertising, is a form of digital advertising where advertisers pay a fee each time their ad is clicked on by a user. This type of advertising is commonly used in search engine advertising, social media advertising, and other forms of online advertising.

In search engine advertising, PPC ads are displayed at the top and bottom of search engine results pages (SERPs). Advertisers bid on specific keywords, and their ad is displayed to users who search for those keywords. The advertiser only pays when a user clicks on their ad, hence the name pay-per-click.

PPC advertising can be a powerful tool for small businesses looking to reach their target audience and drive more business. By targeting specific keywords and audiences, small businesses can reach users who are already searching for their products or services. This can lead to higher click-through rates, more conversions, and ultimately more revenue for the business.

To create an effective PPC campaign, small businesses should start by identifying their target audience and selecting the keywords that they are most likely to search for. They should then create targeted ads that are relevant to those keywords and audiences, and that encourage users to take action, such as making a purchase or signing up for a newsletter.

Another important aspect of creating an effective PPC campaign is tracking and analyzing metrics like click-through rate, conversion rate, and return on investment (ROI). By tracking these metrics, small businesses can identify areas for improvement and adjust their strategy accordingly.

It's important to note that PPC advertising can be complex and time-consuming, particularly for small businesses with limited resources. As such, many small businesses choose to outsource their PPC advertising efforts to a professional agency or freelancer.

PPC advertising can also be expensive, particularly for highly competitive keywords or industries. Small businesses should set a realistic budget for their PPC campaign and adjust it over time based on the results they are seeing.

In addition to search engine advertising, PPC ads can also be used in social media advertising, display advertising, and other forms of online advertising. Each platform has its own unique features and targeting options, and small businesses should choose the platform that best aligns with their target audience and goals.

Finally, it's important to ensure that your PPC advertising efforts are integrated with your overall digital marketing strategy. PPC advertising should be used in conjunction with other digital marketing tactics, such as content creation, social media advertising, and SEO, to create a comprehensive approach that maximizes your reach and effectiveness.

It's important to note that the success of a PPC campaign depends on many factors, including the quality of the ads, the relevancy of the landing pages, and the targeting of the audience. Small businesses should continually monitor their campaigns and make adjustments as necessary to optimize performance and ensure a positive return on investment.

Another important aspect of PPC advertising is ad copywriting. Ad copywriting involves writing compelling and persuasive ad copy that encourages users to click on the ad and take action.

Small businesses should focus on writing ad copy that is relevant to the keywords and audience, and that highlights the unique value proposition of their products or services.

To create effective ad copy, small businesses should focus on benefits over features, use strong calls-to-action, and use emotional appeals when appropriate. They should also use A/B testing to experiment with different ad copy variations and determine which ones are most effective.

In addition to ad copywriting, small businesses should also focus on landing page optimization. The landing page is the page that users are directed to after clicking on the ad, and it plays a critical role in converting clicks into customers. Small businesses should focus on creating landing pages that are relevant to the ad copy and keywords, easy to navigate, and that encourage users to take action.

In conclusion, PPC advertising can be a powerful tool for small businesses looking to reach their target audience and drive more business. By focusing on ad copywriting, landing page optimization, and monitoring performance metrics, small businesses can create an effective and efficient PPC campaign that helps them succeed online. By working with a professional agency, creating compelling ad copy, and optimizing landing pages, small businesses can create a comprehensive PPC advertising strategy that maximizes their reach and impact.

Benefits of PPC advertising for small businesses

PPC advertising offers several benefits to small businesses looking to reach their target audience and drive more business. Here are some of the main benefits of PPC advertising:

Targeted Advertising: With PPC advertising, small businesses can target specific keywords and audiences, ensuring that their ads are shown to users who are most likely to be interested in their products or services. This can lead to higher click-through rates, more conversions, and ultimately more revenue for the business.

Immediate Results: Unlike SEO, which can take months to show results, PPC advertising can generate immediate traffic and results. Small businesses can start seeing results from their PPC campaign as soon as their ads are approved and start running.

Cost-Effective: PPC advertising allows small businesses to set a budget for their campaign and only pay when a user clicks on their ad. This means that small businesses can control their advertising costs and ensure that their marketing budget is being used effectively.

Measurable Results: PPC advertising offers detailed analytics and reporting, allowing small businesses to track the performance of their ads and make data-driven decisions. This can help small businesses identify areas for improvement and optimize their campaign over time for maximum effectiveness.

Flexibility: PPC advertising offers a high degree of flexibility, allowing small businesses to adjust their campaigns based on the results they are seeing. Small businesses can experiment with different ad copy, keywords, and targeting options to find what works best for their business.

In addition to the benefits listed above, PPC advertising also offers small businesses the ability to compete with larger companies. With PPC advertising, small businesses can target the same keywords and audiences as their larger competitors, allowing them to level the playing field and attract customers who might otherwise go to a larger company.

PPC advertising also offers small businesses the ability to test new products or services. By creating targeted campaigns for new products or services, small businesses can test the waters and gauge customer interest before investing in a full marketing campaign.

Finally, PPC advertising can also help small businesses build brand awareness and recognition. By creating ads that showcase their unique value proposition and branding, small businesses can create a strong impression with potential customers and establish themselves as a credible and trustworthy brand.

In conclusion, PPC advertising offers many benefits to small businesses looking to reach their target audience and drive more business. By offering targeted advertising, immediate results, cost-effectiveness, measurable results, flexibility, and the ability to compete with larger companies, PPC advertising can help small businesses succeed online. By using PPC advertising to test new products, build brand awareness, and establish themselves as a credible and trustworthy brand, small businesses can create a comprehensive digital marketing strategy that maximizes their reach and impact.

Google Ads and Facebook Ads platforms

Google Ads and Facebook Ads are two of the most popular platforms for PPC advertising. Here's a closer look at each platform:

Google Ads:

Google Ads is a search engine advertising platform that allows businesses to create ads that appear at the top and bottom of Google search engine results pages (SERPs). Businesses can bid on specific keywords, and their ads are displayed to users who search for those keywords. Google Ads also offers a display advertising network that allows businesses to place ads on websites across the internet.

Google Ads offers several targeting options, including keyword targeting, location targeting, and audience targeting. Businesses can also use Google Ads to create retargeting campaigns that show ads to users who have previously interacted with their website.

One of the key benefits of Google Ads is the ability to target users who are actively searching for a product or service. With keyword targeting, businesses can bid on specific keywords related to their product or service, ensuring that their ads are shown to users who are actively searching for those keywords.

Google Ads also offers several ad formats, including text ads, display ads, shopping ads, and video ads. Text ads are the most common ad format and appear at the top and bottom of search engine results pages (SERPs). Display ads appear on websites across the internet and can be targeted based on specific demographics or interests. Shopping ads allow businesses to showcase their products directly in Google search results, while video ads appear on YouTube and other video-sharing platforms.

Another benefit of Google Ads is the ability to track performance metrics and make data-driven decisions. Google Ads offers detailed analytics and reporting, allowing businesses to track the performance of their ads and make adjustments as necessary to optimize performance and ensure a positive return on investment.

Google Ads also offers several bidding options, including manual bidding and automated bidding. With manual bidding, businesses can set a maximum bid for each keyword, while with automated bidding, Google Ads uses machine learning to adjust bids in real-time based on the likelihood of conversion.

In conclusion, Google Ads is a powerful platform for small businesses looking to reach their target audience and drive more business. By offering keyword targeting, a range of ad formats, detailed analytics and reporting, and bidding options, Google Ads can help small businesses succeed online. By using Google Ads in conjunction with other digital marketing tactics, such as content creation, social media advertising, and SEO, small businesses can create a comprehensive digital marketing strategy that maximizes their reach and impact.

Facebook Ads:

Facebook Ads is a social media advertising platform that allows businesses to create ads that appear in users' Facebook feeds, as well as on other Facebook-owned properties like Instagram and Messenger. Facebook Ads offers several targeting options, including demographic targeting, interest targeting, and behavior targeting.

Facebook Ads also offers a retargeting feature called Custom Audiences, which allows businesses to target users who have interacted with their website, app, or Facebook page. Facebook Ads also offers Lookalike Audiences, which allows businesses to target users who are similar to their existing customers.

One of the key benefits of Facebook Ads is the ability to create highly engaging and visually appealing ads. Facebook Ads allows businesses to use a variety of ad formats, including image ads, video ads, carousel ads, and more.

One of the key benefits of Facebook Ads is the ability to target users based on specific demographics and interests. Facebook Ads offers a range of targeting options, including age, gender, location, interests, behaviors, and more. Businesses can also use Facebook's Custom Audiences feature to target users who have interacted with their website, app, or Facebook page, or Lookalike Audiences to target users who are similar to their existing customers.

Facebook Ads also offers several ad formats, including image ads, video ads, carousel ads, and more. Businesses can use these formats to create highly engaging and visually appealing ads that capture the attention of their target audience.

Another benefit of Facebook Ads is the ability to track performance metrics and make data-driven decisions. Facebook Ads offers detailed analytics and reporting, allowing businesses to track the performance of their ads and make adjustments as necessary to optimize performance and ensure a positive return on investment.

Facebook Ads also offers a range of bidding options, including cost per click (CPC), cost per impression (CPM), and cost per action (CPA). Businesses can choose the bidding option that best fits their goals and budget.

In addition, Facebook Ads offers several tools to help businesses create effective ads, including the Facebook Ad Creative Hub, which allows businesses to create, preview, and test ad creatives before they go live, and the Facebook Ads Manager, which allows businesses to create, manage, and monitor their campaigns.

Facebook Ads is a powerful platform for small businesses looking to reach their target audience and drive more business. By offering a range of targeting options, ad formats, detailed analytics and reporting, and bidding options, Facebook Ads can help small businesses succeed online. By using Facebook Ads in conjunction with other digital marketing tactics, such as content creation, SEO, and email marketing, small businesses can create a comprehensive digital marketing strategy that maximizes their reach and impact.

In conclusion, Google Ads and Facebook Ads are two of the most popular platforms for PPC advertising. While Google Ads offers search engine advertising and display advertising, Facebook Ads offers social media advertising across multiple platforms. Both platforms offer a range of targeting options and retargeting features, allowing businesses to reach their target audience and drive more business. By using both platforms in conjunction with each other, small businesses can create a comprehensive PPC advertising strategy that maximizes their reach and impact.

Creating and managing PPC campaigns

Creating and managing PPC campaigns is a crucial part of digital marketing for small businesses. Here are some steps to follow for creating and managing successful PPC campaigns:

Set Clear Goals: Before creating a PPC campaign, it's important to set clear goals and objectives. This could be anything from generating leads and sales to increasing brand awareness or website traffic.

Conduct Keyword Research: Keyword research is an essential step in creating successful PPC campaigns. It involves identifying the keywords that your target audience is searching for and using those keywords to create targeted ads.

Create Compelling Ads: Ads should be compelling, visually appealing, and include a clear call to action. They should also be tailored to the specific keywords and audience that you're targeting.

Define Targeting Parameters: PPC campaigns offer a range of targeting parameters, including location, demographics, interests, and behaviors. Define these parameters to ensure that your ads are reaching the right audience.

Set Budget and Bids: Determine your advertising budget and set bids for each keyword. This will help you control your advertising costs and ensure that your ads are being shown to users who are most likely to convert.

Monitor and Optimize: Once your campaign is live, monitor its performance and make adjustments as necessary to optimize for maximum effectiveness. This could involve adjusting bids, changing ad copy, or targeting parameters.

Track Performance Metrics: Use analytics and reporting to track the performance of your campaign and make data-driven decisions. Metrics to track include click-through rate, cost per click, conversion rate, and return on investment.

Refine and Improve: Continuously refine and improve your campaign based on performance metrics and user feedback. This will help you maximize your advertising budget and achieve your goals.

In conclusion, creating and managing successful PPC campaigns is an essential part of digital marketing for small businesses. By setting clear goals, conducting keyword research, creating compelling ads, defining targeting parameters, setting budgets and bids, monitoring and optimizing, tracking performance metrics, and refining and improving, small businesses can create effective PPC campaigns that drive more business and help them achieve their marketing goals.

Chapter 7: Content marketing

Importance of content marketing

Content marketing is a digital marketing strategy that involves creating and sharing valuable, relevant, and engaging content with the goal of attracting and retaining a target audience and ultimately driving profitable customer action.

Here are some of the key reasons why content marketing is important for small businesses:

Builds Trust and Authority: By creating valuable and informative content, businesses can establish themselves as experts in their field and build trust with their target audience. This can help increase brand awareness, customer loyalty, and ultimately drive more business.

Improves SEO: Content marketing can also help improve search engine optimization (SEO) by providing search engines with fresh, relevant, and high-quality content to index. This can help businesses rank higher in search engine results pages (SERPs) and drive more organic traffic to their website.

Generates Leads and Sales: Content marketing can also help generate leads and sales by providing potential customers with the information they need to make informed purchasing decisions. By creating content that addresses the needs and pain points of their target audience, businesses can attract and convert more leads into customers.

Increases Engagement: By creating engaging and shareable content, businesses can increase engagement with their target audience and drive more social media shares, likes, and comments. This can help increase brand awareness and ultimately drive more business.

Cost-Effective: Compared to traditional marketing tactics, content marketing is often more cost-effective and can provide a higher return on investment (ROI). By creating content once and repurposing it across multiple channels, businesses can save time and money while still achieving their marketing goals.

Define Target Audience: Before creating content, businesses should define their target audience and understand their needs, interests, and pain points. This can help ensure that the content resonates with the target audience and drives engagement.

Create a Content Plan: Once the target audience is defined, businesses should create a content plan that outlines the types of content to create, the frequency of content creation, and the channels on which to distribute the content.

Create Valuable and Relevant Content: Content should be valuable, relevant, and engaging to the target audience. This could include blog posts, videos, infographics, e-books, and more.

Optimize Content for SEO: Content should be optimized for search engines by including relevant keywords and metadata. This can help improve search engine rankings and drive more organic traffic to the website.

Promote and Distribute Content: Content should be promoted and distributed across multiple channels, including social media, email, and other relevant platforms. This can help increase the reach and engagement of the content.

Measure and Analyze Results: To optimize the content marketing strategy, businesses should measure and analyze the results of their content. This could include metrics such as website traffic, engagement, leads generated, and conversions.

In conclusion, content marketing is a powerful digital marketing strategy that can help small businesses build trust and authority, improve SEO, generate leads and sales, increase engagement, and provide a cost-effective marketing solution. By creating valuable and relevant content that addresses the needs and pain points of their target audience, small businesses can attract and retain more customers and achieve their marketing goals.

Types of content

Content marketing encompasses a wide range of content types, each with its own unique benefits and use cases. Here are some of the most popular types of content for small businesses:

Blog Posts: Blog posts are a popular type of content that can help drive organic traffic to a website. They provide an opportunity to share valuable information and insights on industry topics, showcase expertise, and engage with the target audience.

Videos: Videos are a highly engaging type of content that can help tell a story, showcase products or services, and demonstrate expertise. They can be used for a range of purposes, including product demos, how-to tutorials, and brand storytelling.

Infographics: Infographics are a visual and informative way to communicate complex information in a digestible format. They can be used to share data, statistics, and other information in an easy-to-understand and shareable way.

E-books: E-books are longer-form content pieces that provide in-depth information on a particular topic. They can be used to generate leads and establish authority on a particular subject.

Case Studies: Case studies are a type of content that showcase a particular success story, demonstrating how a business helped solve a problem or achieve a specific goal. They can be used to establish credibility and trust with potential customers.

Whitepapers: Whitepapers are in-depth reports on a particular topic or issue, often featuring original research or analysis. They can be used to provide thought leadership and establish authority on a particular topic.

Social Media Posts: Social media posts are a quick and easy way to engage with the target audience and share valuable information. They can be used to promote blog posts, videos, and other types of content.

By leveraging these different types of content, small businesses can create a diverse and engaging content marketing strategy that resonates with their target audience and achieves their marketing goals. By selecting the most appropriate content types for their target audience and business objectives, small businesses can create a content marketing strategy that drives engagement, generates leads and sales, and helps establish them as thought leaders in their industry.

To ensure that the content marketing strategy is effective, small businesses should also consider the following tips:

Focus on Quality: Quality content is essential for building credibility and trust with the target audience. The content should be well-researched, informative, and provide value to the reader. It should be free of errors and be engaging enough to keep the reader interested.

Be Consistent: Consistency is key when it comes to content marketing. Small businesses should create a content calendar and stick to a regular posting schedule to ensure that the target audience is consistently engaged and interested.

Tailor Content to the Audience: Content should be tailored to the target audience's needs, interests, and preferences. By understanding the target audience's pain points and challenges, small businesses can create content that resonates with them and provides solutions.

Use Visuals: Visuals, such as images, videos, and infographics, can help break up the text and make the content more engaging and shareable. They can also help communicate complex ideas and information in a more digestible format.

Leverage User-Generated Content: User-generated content, such as reviews, testimonials, and social media posts, can help build credibility and trust with the target audience. Small businesses can encourage customers to share their experiences and feedback on social media or other platforms.

Use Analytics: Analytics tools can provide valuable insights into the effectiveness of the content marketing strategy. By tracking metrics such as website traffic, engagement, and conversions, small businesses can refine and improve their content marketing strategy over time.

By following these tips and leveraging the different types of content available, small businesses can create a successful content marketing strategy that drives engagement, generates leads and sales, and helps achieve their marketing goals. With careful planning, regular posting, and ongoing analysis and optimization, small businesses can create a content marketing strategy that provides long-term benefits and establishes them as thought leaders in their industry.

Content creation and distribution strategies

Content creation and distribution are two critical components of a successful content marketing strategy for small businesses.

When it comes to content creation, small businesses need to start by understanding their target audience. They should research their audience's demographics, interests, and pain points to identify relevant topics and create content that resonates with their target audience. This content could take various forms, including blog posts, videos, infographics, e-books, case studies, white papers, and more. Regardless of the content format, it's essential to focus on quality, ensuring that the content is informative, engaging, and valuable to the audience.

Consistency is key when it comes to content creation. Small businesses should create a content calendar and post regularly to keep their target audience engaged and interested. Repurposing content is another effective content creation strategy. Small businesses can take existing content and turn it into a different format to reach new audiences, such as turning a blog post into a video or an infographic.

On the other hand, content distribution is crucial to ensure that the target audience can access the content. Small businesses can use various distribution channels to promote their content, including social media, email marketing, guest blogging, influencer marketing, and paid promotion.

Social media platforms, such as Facebook, Twitter, and LinkedIn, are great places to share content with a broader audience. Small businesses should identify the platforms where their target audience is most active and share relevant content on those platforms. Email marketing is another powerful way to distribute content directly to the target audience. Guest blogging is a strategy where small businesses can create content for other websites or blogs to increase the reach and visibility of their content. Influencer marketing is a way to partner with influencers in their industry to promote their content to a wider audience. Finally, paid promotion, such as social media ads or Google Ads, can help small businesses reach a wider audience and drive more traffic to their website.

By leveraging both content creation and distribution strategies, small businesses can create a successful content marketing strategy that drives engagement, generates leads and sales, and helps achieve their marketing goals. Consistently creating high-quality content, repurposing it across different channels, and distributing it to the target audience can establish small businesses as thought leaders in their industry, attracting and retaining more customers over time.

Content marketing is an important strategy for small businesses because it allows them to establish themselves as thought leaders in their industry and create valuable content that attracts and retains customers. To create effective content, small businesses must first understand their target audience and what types of content will resonate with them. They can then create high-quality content, such as blog posts, videos, and infographics, that is both informative and engaging.

Once the content has been created, small businesses must focus on distribution. Social media is a popular channel for promoting content because it allows small businesses to reach a broad audience quickly. Small businesses can also use email marketing to distribute their content directly to their target audience. Guest blogging is another effective way to increase the reach and visibility of content by leveraging other websites' audiences. Paid promotion, such as social media advertising or Google Ads, can also help small businesses reach a wider audience.

To ensure that their content marketing strategy is effective, small businesses should consider the buyer's journey, tracking metrics using analytics tools, keeping up with trends, and remaining authentic. By creating content that addresses each stage of the buyer's journey, small businesses can move prospects closer to making a purchase. By tracking metrics such as website traffic, engagement, and conversions, small businesses can refine and improve their content marketing strategy over time. Staying up-to-date on trends and best practices can help small businesses remain competitive in their industry. Finally, small businesses should remain authentic to their brand's values and personality to build trust and credibility with their target audience.

By following these steps, small businesses can create a content marketing strategy that drives engagement, generates leads and sales, and establishes them as thought leaders in their industry. With careful planning, regular posting, and ongoing analysis and optimization, small businesses can create a content marketing strategy that provides long-term benefits and contributes to the overall success of their business.

Measuring content marketing success

Measuring the success of a content marketing strategy is crucial for small businesses to determine the effectiveness of their efforts and identify areas for improvement. One of the primary metrics to track is website traffic. By using analytics tools, small businesses can track how many people are visiting their website, which pages are being visited, and how long people are staying on the site. A higher number of website visitors indicates that the content is attracting people to the site, but it's important to also look at the quality of the traffic. For example, if the bounce rate is high, it may indicate that the content isn't meeting the audience's expectations.

Engagement metrics are also important to track. Social media likes, shares, and comments can indicate how well the content is resonating with the audience. High engagement metrics demonstrate that the content is valuable and engaging, which can lead to more visibility and more significant reach.

Small businesses should also track the conversion rate, which is the percentage of website visitors who take a specific action, such as filling out a contact form or making a purchase. A high conversion rate means that the content is effectively encouraging prospects to take the desired action.

For businesses that use email marketing, tracking subscriber growth is essential. A growing email list is a strong indicator of the content's success and can lead to more sales and revenue over time. Brand awareness is another metric to track, which can be done by monitoring mentions of the brand on social media or tracking how many people are searching for the brand online.

It's important to keep in mind that content marketing is a long-term strategy, and it may take time to see results. It's crucial to consistently track these metrics over time to determine the effectiveness of the content marketing strategy and make adjustments as needed to improve the results.

In addition to these primary metrics, small businesses should also track other relevant metrics that align with their specific goals and objectives. For example, if the goal is to increase brand awareness, tracking social media followers or website mentions may be relevant. On the other hand, if the goal is to increase sales, tracking revenue or conversion rate may be more important.

It's also essential to track metrics on an ongoing basis to determine how the content marketing strategy is performing over time. Small businesses should regularly review their metrics to identify trends and patterns and adjust their strategy as necessary to improve results.

Finally, small businesses should consider benchmarking their metrics against industry standards to understand how their content marketing strategy compares to their competitors. This can provide valuable insights into the effectiveness of the strategy and identify areas for improvement.

In summary, measuring content marketing success involves tracking relevant metrics on an ongoing basis, adjusting the strategy as needed, and benchmarking against industry standards. By consistently tracking and analyzing these metrics, small businesses can improve their content marketing strategy and achieve their marketing goals.

Chapter 8: Influencer marketing

Definition and importance of influencer marketing

Influencer marketing is a marketing strategy that involves partnering with influential people in a particular industry or niche to promote a product or service. Influencers are people with a significant following on social media platforms, such as Instagram, YouTube, or TikTok, who have built trust and credibility with their followers. Influencer marketing involves working with these individuals to create content that promotes a brand, product, or service to their followers.

The importance of influencer marketing for small businesses lies in the ability to leverage the trust and credibility that influencers have built with their followers. By partnering with influencers, small businesses can reach a highly targeted audience and build brand awareness quickly. Additionally, influencer marketing can help small businesses increase their reach, engagement, and ultimately, sales.

Influencer marketing is particularly effective for small businesses that are targeting a specific niche or demographic. For example, a small business that sells vegan protein powder can partner with a fitness influencer who is also vegan to promote their product to a highly targeted audience. This type of collaboration can help small businesses reach potential customers who are interested in their product and are more likely to convert.

Another advantage of influencer marketing for small businesses is the ability to create authentic and engaging content. Influencers are skilled at creating content that resonates with their followers and can help small businesses create content that is both informative and engaging. Additionally, influencer marketing can help small businesses build relationships with their target audience by leveraging the influencer's personal brand and story.

Influencer marketing is a powerful marketing strategy that allows small businesses to reach a highly targeted audience, build brand awareness quickly, and create authentic and engaging content. By partnering with influencers who have built trust and credibility with their followers, small businesses can increase their reach, engagement, and ultimately, sales.

To successfully implement an influencer marketing campaign, small businesses should first identify the right influencers to partner with. This involves researching influencers who align with the brand's values, target audience, and goals. Small businesses should also consider factors such as the influencer's engagement rate, reach, and demographics to ensure that they are reaching the right audience.

Once the influencers are identified, small businesses should work with them to develop a content strategy that aligns with the brand's messaging and goals. This may involve providing the influencer with product samples or creative briefs to guide the content creation process. It's essential to establish clear guidelines and expectations to ensure that the content is on-brand and aligns with the campaign's objectives.

Another critical aspect of influencer marketing is measuring the campaign's success. Small businesses should establish clear metrics to track the campaign's performance, such as engagement rate, reach, conversions, and revenue. This allows small businesses to determine the effectiveness of the campaign and make adjustments as needed to improve results.

Influencer marketing is a powerful marketing strategy that can help small businesses reach a highly targeted audience, build brand awareness quickly, and create authentic and engaging content. To successfully implement an influencer marketing campaign, small businesses should identify the right influencers, develop a content strategy, measure the campaign's success, and nurture long-term relationships with influencers. By leveraging the trust and credibility that influencers have built with their followers, small businesses can increase their reach, engagement, and ultimately, sales.

It's worth noting that influencer marketing is not without its challenges. One of the biggest challenges for small businesses is finding the right influencers who are both a good fit for the brand and have a genuine following. Some influencers may have purchased followers or engagement, which can result in a less effective campaign.

Another challenge is ensuring that the content created by influencers aligns with the brand's messaging and values. Small businesses need to establish clear guidelines and expectations to ensure that the content is on-brand and resonates with the target audience.

In addition, influencer marketing can be expensive, particularly if small businesses are working with well-known influencers who command high fees. Small businesses need to carefully consider their budget and the potential return on investment when deciding to pursue influencer marketing.

Despite these challenges, influencer marketing can be a highly effective marketing strategy for small businesses when done correctly. By identifying the right influencers, developing a content strategy, measuring the campaign's success, and nurturing long-term relationships with influencers, small businesses can leverage the trust and credibility that influencers have built with their followers to increase their reach, engagement, and ultimately, sales.

Finding the right influencers for your brand

Finding the right influencers for your brand is critical to the success of your influencer marketing campaign. It's important to identify influencers who have a genuine following and align with your brand's values, target audience, and goals.

The first step in finding the right influencers is to identify your target audience. Who are the people you want to reach with your campaign? What social media platforms do they use, and what types of content do they engage with? Once you have a clear understanding of your target audience, you can begin searching for influencers who align with those demographics.

There are several tools available to help you find influencers in your niche or industry. Social media platforms such as Instagram and TikTok have built-in search functions that allow you to search for influencers by keywords, hashtags, and location. You can also use influencer marketing platforms such as AspireIQ, Grin, or Upfluence, which provide access to a network of influencers and can help you manage your campaigns.

When evaluating potential influencers, it's essential to look beyond their follower count and engagement rate. While these metrics are important, they don't necessarily indicate an influencer's effectiveness. Instead, look for influencers who have built trust and credibility with their followers, are passionate about your industry or niche, and are a good fit for your brand.

You can also use metrics such as reach, engagement rate, and demographics to evaluate influencers. These metrics can help you determine whether an influencer is reaching your target audience and can provide insights into the effectiveness of their content.

It's also important to establish clear guidelines and expectations when working with influencers. This can include providing them with creative briefs or product samples, outlining the campaign objectives and messaging, and setting expectations for deliverables and timelines.

Another factor to consider when evaluating potential influencers is their authenticity. Influencers who are authentic and genuine are more likely to resonate with their followers and build trust and credibility. Look for influencers who share your brand's values and are passionate about your industry or niche.

In addition to evaluating potential influencers, small businesses should also consider the type of partnership they want to establish with influencers. This can include one-off collaborations or longer-term partnerships, such as brand ambassadors. Longer-term partnerships can be more effective in building relationships with influencers and creating ongoing content that resonates with your target audience.

Finally, small businesses should track the success of their influencer marketing campaigns and make adjustments as needed. This can involve measuring metrics such as engagement rate, reach, conversions, and revenue, and making changes to the campaign strategy based on the results.

In summary, finding the right influencers for your brand involves identifying your target audience, evaluating potential influencers based on factors such as trust, authenticity, and fit with your brand, establishing clear guidelines and expectations, considering the type of partnership you want to establish, and tracking the success of your campaigns. By leveraging the power of influencer marketing, small businesses can reach a highly targeted audience, build brand awareness quickly, and create authentic and engaging content that resonates with their target audience.

Building relationships with influencers

Building relationships with influencers is an essential aspect of influencer marketing for small businesses. Long-term partnerships can be more effective in creating ongoing content that resonates with your target audience and helps build brand awareness and credibility.

To build relationships with influencers, small businesses should start by reaching out to potential partners and introducing themselves and their brand. This can involve sending an email or direct message, expressing interest in collaborating with the influencer, and sharing information about the brand and the campaign objectives.

It's important to establish clear guidelines and expectations for the partnership, including the types of content that will be created, the frequency of collaborations, and the compensation or incentives offered to the influencer. This can help ensure that the partnership is mutually beneficial and aligns with the influencer's values and goals.

Small businesses can also foster relationships with influencers by engaging with their content and sharing it on their own social media channels. This can help increase the influencer's reach and build goodwill between the brand and the influencer.

Another effective strategy for building relationships with influencers is to offer exclusive content or opportunities. This can include providing the influencer with exclusive access to a product launch or event, or offering them the opportunity to create sponsored content that aligns with their personal brand.

It's important to maintain regular communication with influencers and show appreciation for their contributions to the campaign. This can involve providing feedback on their content, sharing their content with your own followers, and offering incentives or rewards for their efforts.

In addition to the strategies mentioned above, small businesses can also leverage the power of micro-influencers to build relationships and reach highly targeted audiences. Micro-influencers typically have smaller followings but are highly engaged with their audience and have built trust and credibility in their niche or industry. They can be more affordable for small businesses and can be an effective way to reach niche or highly targeted audiences.

To build relationships with micro-influencers, small businesses can start by identifying influencers who align with their brand's values and target audience. They can then reach out to these influencers and offer opportunities to collaborate on campaigns or create sponsored content. Small businesses can also engage with micro-influencers' content, share it with their own followers, and offer incentives or rewards for their efforts.

Another effective strategy for building relationships with influencers is to provide them with value beyond just compensation or exposure. This can involve offering them access to exclusive products or services, providing them with industry insights or networking opportunities, or offering them opportunities for personal or professional development.

It's also important to be authentic and transparent when working with influencers. This can involve providing them with creative control over the content they create, disclosing sponsored content to their audience, and being honest and transparent about the partnership and compensation.

Maintaining a positive relationship with influencers is crucial for the long-term success of influencer marketing campaigns. Small businesses should aim to create a collaborative environment with influencers and ensure that they feel valued and appreciated for their contributions.

Regular communication is key to maintaining a positive relationship with influencers. Small businesses should keep influencers informed about campaign updates and provide feedback on their content. They should also be available to answer any questions or concerns that influencers may have throughout the campaign.

Small businesses can also foster a positive relationship with influencers by offering incentives or rewards for their efforts. This can include compensation for sponsored content, access to exclusive products or services, or invitations to industry events or networking opportunities.

Another effective strategy for maintaining a positive relationship with influencers is to provide them with constructive feedback on their content. This can help improve the quality and effectiveness of the content and can help build trust and credibility between the influencer and the brand.

Finally, it's important to show appreciation for the influencer's contributions to the campaign. This can involve sharing their content with your own followers, featuring them on your website or social media channels, or offering them public recognition for their efforts.

In summary, building relationships with influencers involves reaching out to potential partners, establishing clear guidelines and expectations, engaging with their content, offering exclusive opportunities, maintaining regular communication, and showing appreciation for their contributions. By building long-term relationships with influencers, small businesses can create ongoing collaborations that resonate with their target audience and drive brand awareness and credibility.

Measuring influencer marketing success

Measuring the success of influencer marketing campaigns is crucial for small businesses to understand the effectiveness of their campaigns and make adjustments as needed. There are several key metrics that can be used to measure the success of influencer marketing campaigns.

One of the most important metrics is engagement rate. Engagement rate measures how many people interact with the influencer's content, including likes, comments, and shares. A high engagement rate indicates that the content resonates with the audience and is effective in driving brand awareness and engagement.

Another important metric is reach, which measures how many people are exposed to the influencer's content. Reach is an important indicator of the campaign's overall reach and potential impact.

Conversion rate is another important metric to measure the success of influencer marketing campaigns. Conversion rate measures how many people take a desired action, such as making a purchase or signing up for a newsletter, after seeing the influencer's content.

In addition to these metrics, small businesses should also track revenue generated from the campaign and monitor brand sentiment and reputation online.

To measure the success of influencer marketing campaigns, small businesses can use a variety of tools and platforms. Social media analytics tools can provide insights into engagement rate, reach, and conversion rate, while revenue tracking tools can help measure the financial impact of the campaign.

It's important to measure the success of influencer marketing campaigns regularly and make adjustments as needed. This can involve tweaking the campaign strategy or targeting different audiences based on the results.

In addition to tracking metrics, small businesses should also consider the qualitative impact of their influencer marketing campaigns. This includes evaluating the quality and relevance of the content created by influencers, the level of engagement and interaction with the audience, and the overall impact on the brand's reputation and credibility.

Small businesses can also use surveys or focus groups to gather feedback from their target audience about the influencer marketing campaign. This feedback can provide valuable insights into the effectiveness of the campaign and areas for improvement.

Another important aspect of measuring influencer marketing success is tracking the return on investment (ROI) of the campaign. This involves measuring the financial impact of the campaign by calculating the revenue generated by the campaign and comparing it to the cost of the campaign, including compensation for influencers and any other associated costs.

Calculating ROI can help small businesses make data-driven decisions about their influencer marketing strategies and adjust their approach to maximize their return on investment.

It's important to note that measuring the success of influencer marketing campaigns can be challenging, and results may vary depending on factors such as the influencer's audience, the type of content created, and the overall marketing strategy. As such, small businesses should approach influencer marketing as a long-term strategy and be prepared to make adjustments and optimizations as needed.

In summary, measuring the success of influencer marketing campaigns involves evaluating both quantitative and qualitative metrics, including engagement rate, reach, conversion rate, brand sentiment, and ROI. By tracking these metrics and gathering feedback from the audience, small businesses can make data-driven decisions about their influencer marketing strategies and maximize their impact on brand awareness, credibility, and sales.

Chapter 9: Affiliate marketing

Definition and importance of affiliate marketing

Affiliate marketing is a performance-based marketing strategy in which a business rewards affiliates for each customer or sale that they bring to the business. Affiliates promote the business's products or services to their own audience through various channels such as social media, blogs, or email marketing. When a customer makes a purchase through the affiliate's unique referral link, the affiliate earns a commission on the sale.

Affiliate marketing is important for small businesses as it allows them to reach new audiences and drive sales without incurring upfront costs. Unlike traditional advertising methods, small businesses only pay affiliates when they generate sales or leads, making it a cost-effective way to drive traffic and sales.

Affiliate marketing can also help small businesses build brand awareness and credibility by leveraging the trust and authority of affiliates. Affiliates who have built a loyal following and established credibility in their niche or industry can be powerful advocates for small businesses, helping to increase brand awareness and drive sales.

Another benefit of affiliate marketing is that it allows small businesses to tap into the expertise and creativity of affiliates. Affiliates are often experts in their niche or industry and can provide valuable insights and feedback on the business's products or services. They can also offer creative ideas for marketing campaigns and promotions that can help small businesses stand out in a crowded market.

To effectively implement affiliate marketing, small businesses should first identify their target audience and the types of affiliates that would be a good fit for their brand. This involves researching potential affiliates, evaluating their reach and credibility, and determining whether their audience aligns with the business's target audience.

Once the right affiliates have been identified, small businesses should develop an affiliate marketing program that offers competitive commission rates, clear guidelines and expectations, and effective promotional materials. This can include providing affiliates with exclusive discounts, access to new products or services, and creative content such as images and videos that they can use to promote the business.

Small businesses should also establish clear communication channels with their affiliates and provide them with regular updates and support throughout the campaign. This can involve providing feedback on their content, answering questions and concerns, and offering guidance on best practices for promoting the business.

To measure the success of their affiliate marketing program, small businesses should track key metrics such as clicks, conversions, and revenue generated through affiliate referrals. They should also regularly evaluate the effectiveness of their affiliate partnerships and make adjustments as needed based on the results.

It's important to note that affiliate marketing is not a one-size-fits-all solution and may not be the right fit for every small business. It requires a strategic approach, careful planning, and ongoing management to be successful.

Small businesses should also be aware of potential pitfalls associated with affiliate marketing, such as the risk of fraudulent activity or negative brand associations with certain affiliates. As such, it's important for small businesses to carefully vet potential affiliates and establish clear guidelines and expectations to ensure that their brand is being promoted in a way that aligns with their values and goals.

In summary, affiliate marketing is a powerful strategy for small businesses to reach new audiences, drive sales, and build brand awareness and credibility. By identifying the right affiliates, developing a competitive commission structure, providing effective promotional materials and support, and regularly evaluating the effectiveness of the program, small businesses can leverage the power of affiliate marketing to grow their business and reach their goals.

Setting up an affiliate program

Setting up an affiliate program involves several key steps to ensure that the program is effective and successful. These steps include:

Defining the commission structure: Small businesses should decide on the commission structure that will be offered to affiliates. This can include a percentage of each sale or a flat fee for each referral.

Identifying potential affiliates: Small businesses should identify potential affiliates that are a good fit for their brand and target audience. This can involve researching influencers, bloggers, and other individuals or companies that have a relevant audience.

Developing promotional materials: Small businesses should develop effective promotional materials such as banner ads, text links, and other creative content that affiliates can use to promote the business.

Establishing clear guidelines and expectations: Small businesses should establish clear guidelines and expectations for affiliates, including rules around using the business's brand name, messaging, and imagery. This can help ensure that the business's brand is being promoted in a way that aligns with its values and goals.

Setting up tracking and reporting: Small businesses should set up tracking and reporting tools to monitor the success of their affiliate program. This can include tracking clicks, conversions, and revenue generated through affiliate referrals.

Providing support and communication: Small businesses should establish clear communication channels with their affiliates and provide them with regular updates and support throughout the program.

Regularly evaluating and adjusting the program: Small businesses should regularly evaluate the effectiveness of their affiliate program and make adjustments as needed based on the results.

Overall, setting up an affiliate program requires careful planning, effective communication, and ongoing management to ensure that the program is successful. By following these steps, small businesses can leverage the power of affiliate marketing to reach new audiences, drive sales, and build brand awareness and credibility.

Small businesses can also use affiliate network platforms to help them set up and manage their affiliate program. These platforms provide a centralized platform for businesses to manage their affiliate relationships and provide tools for tracking clicks, conversions, and other key metrics.

When selecting an affiliate network platform, small businesses should consider factors such as the platform's fees, ease of use, and available features such as reporting and communication tools. Popular affiliate network platforms include ShareASale, CJ Affiliate, and Rakuten Marketing.

In addition to using affiliate network platforms, small businesses can also use affiliate marketing software to manage their program. Affiliate marketing software provides businesses with tools for tracking clicks and conversions, creating custom commission structures, and managing communication with affiliates. Popular affiliate marketing software options include Refersion, Post Affiliate Pro, and AffiliateWP.

To ensure the success of their affiliate program, small businesses should also regularly evaluate and adjust their commission structure, promotional materials, and communication strategy based on the results of their tracking and reporting. This can help ensure that the program is effective in driving sales and building brand awareness.

Setting up an affiliate program involves several key steps, including defining the commission structure, identifying potential affiliates, developing promotional materials, establishing clear guidelines and expectations, setting up tracking and reporting, providing support and communication, and regularly evaluating and adjusting the program. By following these steps and leveraging the tools provided by affiliate network platforms and software, small businesses can successfully implement an affiliate marketing strategy to drive sales and build their brand.

It's important for small businesses to remember that implementing an effective affiliate program requires ongoing management and support. This includes providing affiliates with regular updates and promotions, offering feedback on their content and promotions, and addressing any concerns or questions that they may have.

Small businesses should also be aware of potential challenges that may arise when managing an affiliate program, such as fraudulent activity or negative brand associations with certain affiliates. As such, it's important to carefully vet potential affiliates and establish clear guidelines and expectations to ensure that the program is effective and aligned with the business's values and goals.

Overall, implementing an affiliate program can be a powerful strategy for small businesses to drive sales, reach new audiences, and build brand awareness and credibility. By carefully planning and executing the program, providing ongoing support and management, and regularly evaluating and adjusting the program based on results, small businesses can successfully leverage the power of affiliate marketing to achieve their goals.

Finding and recruiting affiliates

Finding and recruiting affiliates is a critical component of a successful affiliate marketing program. Small businesses can use a variety of methods to find and recruit potential affiliates, including:

Search engines: One of the easiest ways to find potential affiliates is by searching for relevant keywords in search engines such as Google. This can help businesses identify bloggers, influencers, and other websites that are relevant to their industry or target audience.

Social media: Small businesses can also use social media platforms such as Twitter and LinkedIn to search for potential affiliates. By searching for relevant hashtags and keywords, businesses can identify individuals or companies that are actively engaged in their industry or niche.

Affiliate networks: Affiliate networks such as ShareASale and CJ Affiliate provide a centralized platform for businesses to connect with potential affiliates. These platforms allow businesses to browse through a list of potential affiliates and filter them based on various criteria such as audience size, niche, and geographic location.

Existing customers: Small businesses can also leverage their existing customer base to recruit affiliates. By offering incentives such as discounts or free products, businesses can encourage their customers to refer others to their program.

Once potential affiliates have been identified, small businesses should reach out to them and provide them with information about the program. This can include details such as the commission structure, promotional materials, and any guidelines or expectations that the business may have.

To recruit affiliates effectively, small businesses should also consider offering incentives such as competitive commission rates, bonuses for high performers, and access to exclusive promotions or content. By providing these incentives, businesses can attract high-quality affiliates who are motivated to promote their products or services.

In addition to finding and recruiting affiliates, small businesses should also establish clear guidelines and expectations for their affiliates. This can include guidelines on how affiliates can promote their products or services, what types of content they can use, and any restrictions or limitations that may apply.

Small businesses should also provide their affiliates with promotional materials such as banners, text links, and email templates that they can use to promote their products or services. By providing these materials, businesses can ensure that their affiliates are promoting their brand in a consistent and effective manner.

To effectively manage their affiliates, small businesses should also provide regular communication and support. This can include providing affiliates with regular updates on new products or promotions, answering any questions or concerns they may have, and providing feedback on their promotional efforts.

Small businesses should also track and measure the performance of their affiliate program. This can include tracking clicks, conversions, and other key metrics to determine the effectiveness of the program and identify areas for improvement. By regularly analyzing this data, small businesses can make informed decisions about how to optimize their affiliate program to achieve their marketing goals.

Finding and recruiting affiliates is an important aspect of building a successful affiliate marketing program. By using a variety of methods to identify potential affiliates, establishing clear guidelines and expectations, providing promotional materials and support, and regularly tracking and measuring performance, small businesses can effectively leverage the power of affiliate marketing to drive sales and build their brand.

Measuring affiliate marketing success

Measuring the success of an affiliate marketing program is crucial for small businesses to determine whether the program is effective in driving sales and achieving their marketing goals. Here are some key metrics that small businesses can use to measure the success of their affiliate marketing program:

Clicks: Tracking the number of clicks on affiliate links or banners can help small businesses determine how effective their promotional materials are in driving traffic to their website.

Conversions: Measuring the number of conversions or sales generated by the affiliate program can help businesses determine the program's overall effectiveness in driving revenue.

Average order value (AOV): Calculating the average order value of sales generated by the affiliate program can help small businesses determine whether their affiliates are driving higher-value sales.

Return on investment (ROI): Calculating the ROI of the affiliate program can help small businesses determine whether the program is generating a positive return on investment.

Cost per acquisition (CPA): Measuring the cost per acquisition of each sale generated by the affiliate program can help small businesses determine the profitability of the program.

Affiliate performance: Tracking the performance of individual affiliates can help small businesses identify their top performers and incentivize them to continue promoting their products or services.

Small businesses should also regularly analyze and evaluate these metrics to identify areas for improvement and optimize their affiliate marketing program. This can include adjusting the commission structure, providing new promotional materials, or targeting new audiences.

In addition to these metrics, small businesses should also consider qualitative factors such as brand awareness, audience engagement, and customer loyalty when measuring the success of their affiliate marketing program. These factors can provide insights into the program's overall impact on the business's brand and reputation.

Small businesses can use a variety of tools and technologies to measure the success of their affiliate marketing program. Affiliate networks such as ShareASale and CJ Affiliate provide built-in tracking and reporting tools that allow businesses to track clicks, conversions, and other key metrics.

Additionally, small businesses can use analytics platforms such as Google Analytics to track and measure the effectiveness of their affiliate program. By setting up custom tracking parameters and goals, businesses can track the performance of individual affiliates and identify areas for improvement.

To further optimize their affiliate program, small businesses can also use A/B testing to test different promotional materials and commission structures. By comparing the performance of different variations, businesses can identify which approaches are most effective in driving traffic and sales.

It's also important for small businesses to establish clear goals and benchmarks for their affiliate marketing program. This can include setting specific targets for clicks, conversions, or revenue generated by the program. By setting clear goals and regularly measuring their progress towards them, small businesses can determine whether their affiliate program is on track to achieve their marketing goals.

Overall, measuring the success of an affiliate marketing program requires careful tracking and analysis of key metrics, as well as a commitment to ongoing optimization and improvement. By using a variety of tools and technologies to track performance, establish clear goals and benchmarks, and continually test and optimize promotional materials and commission structures, small businesses can build a successful affiliate marketing program that drives sales and builds their brand.

Chapter 10: Analytics and measurement

Importance of analytics and measurement

Analytics and measurement are crucial components of digital marketing for small businesses. They allow businesses to track and measure the effectiveness of their marketing campaigns and make data-driven decisions to optimize their strategies and achieve their goals.

One of the key benefits of analytics and measurement is that they provide businesses with valuable insights into customer behavior and preferences. By tracking metrics such as website traffic, engagement rates, and conversion rates, businesses can gain a better understanding of their target audience and tailor their marketing strategies to better meet their needs.

Analytics and measurement also enable businesses to identify areas for improvement in their marketing campaigns. By analyzing data on key performance indicators (KPIs) such as click-through rates, bounce rates, and time on site, businesses can identify which aspects of their campaigns are working well and which areas need improvement. This can help businesses refine their strategies and optimize their marketing efforts to achieve better results.

Another important benefit of analytics and measurement is that they enable businesses to track their return on investment (ROI) for their marketing campaigns. By tracking the costs of their campaigns and measuring the revenue generated by their efforts, businesses can determine whether their marketing strategies are generating a positive ROI and adjust their budgets accordingly.

Overall, analytics and measurement are essential for small businesses looking to succeed in the competitive world of digital marketing. By using data to gain insights into customer behavior, identify areas for improvement, and track their ROI, businesses can optimize their marketing strategies and achieve better results.

Analytics and measurement can be used across a variety of digital marketing channels and strategies, including search engine optimization (SEO), pay-per-click (PPC) advertising, social media marketing, email marketing, content marketing, and more.

For example, in SEO, businesses can use analytics tools such as Google Analytics to track website traffic, search engine rankings, and other key metrics. By analyzing this data, businesses can identify which keywords and pages are driving the most traffic and adjust their SEO strategies accordingly.

In PPC advertising, businesses can use analytics to track clicks, conversions, and other metrics to determine the effectiveness of their campaigns. By analyzing this data, businesses can identify which ads and keywords are performing the best and adjust their campaigns to improve their results.

Similarly, in social media marketing, businesses can use analytics tools such as Facebook Insights to track engagement rates, reach, and other metrics. By analyzing this data, businesses can identify which types of content and messaging are resonating with their target audience and adjust their social media strategies accordingly.

In email marketing, businesses can use analytics to track open rates, click-through rates, and other metrics to determine the effectiveness of their campaigns. By analyzing this data, businesses can identify which subject lines, messaging, and calls-to-action are driving the most engagement and adjust their email marketing strategies accordingly.

Overall, the use of analytics and measurement is essential for small businesses looking to succeed in digital marketing. By tracking and analyzing key metrics across their various marketing channels and strategies, businesses can gain valuable insights into their audience, refine their messaging and strategies, and ultimately achieve better results and a higher ROI.

It's important to note that analytics and measurement go beyond simply tracking metrics and numbers. They also involve analyzing and interpreting data to gain actionable insights that can inform future marketing strategies and campaigns.

For example, by analyzing customer behavior data, businesses can identify patterns and trends in how their target audience interacts with their website or social media accounts. This can help them make informed decisions about website design and content, or adjust their social media strategy to better engage their audience.

Analytics and measurement can also help businesses identify opportunities for growth and expansion. By identifying which marketing channels and strategies are driving the most traffic, engagement, and sales, businesses can focus their resources on these areas to maximize their impact.

Moreover, analytics and measurement can help businesses understand the effectiveness of their marketing campaigns in the context of their overall business goals. By tracking metrics such as customer lifetime value or average order value, businesses can determine the impact of their marketing efforts on revenue and profitability.

In summary, analytics and measurement are essential for small businesses to make informed decisions about their digital marketing strategies. By tracking and analyzing key metrics across their various marketing channels and strategies, businesses can gain valuable insights into customer behavior, identify opportunities for growth and expansion, and understand the effectiveness of their marketing efforts in the context of their overall business goals.

Google Analytics and other tools

Google Analytics is a popular and powerful analytics tool that businesses can use to track and analyze website traffic and user behavior. It provides businesses with a wealth of information about their website visitors, including demographic information, location, interests, and behavior.

In addition to Google Analytics, there are many other analytics tools available that businesses can use to track and measure the effectiveness of their digital marketing campaigns. Some examples include:

Adobe Analytics: A comprehensive analytics tool that provides businesses with a range of data and insights about their website visitors, including behavior, engagement, and conversion data.

SEMrush: A popular tool for SEO and PPC analytics, SEMrush provides businesses with detailed insights into keyword rankings, website traffic, and ad performance.

Ahrefs: A powerful SEO tool that provides businesses with insights into backlinks, keyword rankings, and website traffic.

Hootsuite Insights: A social media analytics tool that enables businesses to track engagement, sentiment, and other metrics across multiple social media platforms.

Mailchimp: An email marketing platform that provides businesses with data on open rates, click-through rates, and other key metrics for their email campaigns.

In addition to these dedicated analytics tools, many digital marketing platforms also offer built-in analytics and reporting features. For example, social media platforms such as Facebook and Twitter provide businesses with insights into engagement rates, reach, and other key metrics for their social media campaigns.

Similarly, email marketing platforms like Mailchimp and Constant Contact offer built-in analytics features that enable businesses to track and measure the effectiveness of their email campaigns. These features can provide businesses with data on open rates, click-through rates, and other key metrics for their email campaigns.

Overall, the use of analytics tools and features is essential for small businesses looking to succeed in digital marketing. By tracking and analyzing key metrics across their various marketing channels and strategies, businesses can gain valuable insights into their audience, refine their messaging and strategies, and ultimately achieve better results and a higher ROI.

Setting goals and KPIs

Setting goals and KPIs (key performance indicators) is essential for small businesses to measure the success of their digital marketing efforts. Goals and KPIs help businesses define what success looks like for their marketing campaigns, and provide a clear roadmap for achieving it.

To set effective goals and KPIs, businesses should start by defining their overall business objectives. For example, a small business might have a goal of increasing revenue, growing their customer base, or improving brand awareness. Once these objectives have been established, businesses can then set specific goals and KPIs for their digital marketing efforts that align with these objectives.

For example, if a small business's goal is to increase revenue, they might set a KPI of increasing website traffic, or improving their website's conversion rate. Alternatively, if the goal is to improve brand awareness, they might set a KPI of increasing social media engagement, or improving their search engine rankings.

When setting goals and KPIs, it's important to make sure they are SMART: specific, measurable, attainable, relevant, and time-bound. This means that goals and KPIs should be specific and clearly defined, measurable and quantifiable, achievable within a reasonable timeframe, relevant to the overall business objectives, and tied to a specific timeline or deadline.

Once goals and KPIs have been established, businesses should track and measure their progress regularly. This can be done using tools like Google Analytics or social media analytics, or through manual tracking and reporting. By regularly measuring and analyzing their performance against their goals and KPIs, businesses can make informed decisions about their digital marketing strategies, and make adjustments as needed to achieve better results.

In addition to tracking and measuring progress against goals and KPIs, businesses should also regularly review and analyze their data to gain insights into their audience and the effectiveness of their marketing strategies. This can involve analyzing user behavior on their website or social media platforms, tracking the performance of individual campaigns, and identifying trends and patterns in user engagement and conversion.

By regularly reviewing and analyzing this data, businesses can identify areas of strength and weakness in their digital marketing strategies, and make informed decisions about how to optimize and improve their campaigns. For example, they might identify a particular social media platform that is driving significant traffic and engagement, and decide to allocate more resources to that platform. Alternatively, they might identify a specific type of content or messaging that is resonating particularly well with their audience, and adjust their strategy accordingly.

Ultimately, setting goals and KPIs, and regularly tracking and analyzing data, is essential for small businesses looking to succeed in digital marketing. By using data to inform their strategies and make informed decisions, businesses can achieve better results, improve their ROI, and ultimately grow and succeed in today's digital marketplace.

Measuring digital marketing success and ROI

Measuring digital marketing success and ROI (return on investment) is crucial for small businesses to determine the effectiveness and profitability of their marketing efforts. To accurately measure success and ROI, businesses should track and analyze a variety of key metrics and data points across their various marketing channels and strategies.

Some common metrics that businesses might track include website traffic, engagement rates on social media, email open rates and click-through rates, search engine rankings, and conversion rates (such as the number of leads generated or products sold). By tracking these metrics, businesses can gain valuable insights into the effectiveness of their marketing efforts, and make informed decisions about how to optimize and improve their campaigns.

In addition to tracking metrics, businesses should also calculate their ROI for each marketing campaign or strategy. To calculate ROI, businesses should compare the revenue generated from a particular campaign or strategy to the total cost of that campaign (including any advertising spend or other expenses). This calculation can help businesses determine whether a particular campaign or strategy is generating a positive return on investment, and can inform future investment and resource allocation decisions.

It's important to note that measuring digital marketing success and ROI is an ongoing process, and requires regular tracking and analysis. By regularly reviewing and analyzing data, businesses can identify areas of strength and weakness in their marketing strategies, and make informed decisions about how to optimize and improve their campaigns for maximum ROI.

Overall, measuring digital marketing success and ROI is essential for small businesses looking to succeed in today's competitive digital landscape. By tracking metrics and calculating ROI, businesses can gain valuable insights into the effectiveness of their marketing efforts, and make informed decisions about how to allocate their resources for maximum impact and profitability.

To effectively measure digital marketing success and ROI, businesses can use a variety of tools and techniques. Here are some examples:

Google Analytics: Google Analytics is a free web analytics tool that provides businesses with detailed information about website traffic, user behavior, and conversion rates. By tracking metrics such as bounce rates, time on site, and goal completions, businesses can gain valuable insights into the effectiveness of their website and marketing strategies.

Social media analytics: Most social media platforms provide businesses with analytics tools that allow them to track engagement rates, reach, and audience demographics. By tracking these metrics, businesses can identify which platforms and types of content are resonating most with their audience, and make informed decisions about how to optimize their social media strategies.

Email marketing analytics: Email marketing platforms like Mailchimp or Constant Contact provide businesses with detailed information about email open rates, click-through rates, and conversion rates. By tracking these metrics, businesses can identify which types of content and messaging are most effective, and make informed decisions about how to optimize their email marketing campaigns.

Conversion tracking: Conversion tracking tools allow businesses to track the number of leads generated or products sold as a result of a particular marketing campaign. By setting up conversion tracking on their website or landing pages, businesses can determine the ROI of their campaigns and make informed decisions about how to optimize their marketing strategies for maximum impact.

Ultimately, measuring digital marketing success and ROI requires a commitment to regular tracking and analysis of data across multiple channels and platforms. By using these tools and techniques, businesses can gain valuable insights into the effectiveness of their marketing efforts, and make informed decisions about how to optimize and improve their strategies for maximum impact and profitability.

Chapter 11: Creating a digital marketing plan

Importance of having a digital marketing plan

In today's digital age, having a digital marketing plan is crucial for small businesses looking to succeed in the competitive digital marketplace. A digital marketing plan outlines a comprehensive strategy for promoting products or services, building brand awareness, and engaging with customers across multiple digital channels.

Here are some reasons why having a digital marketing plan is essential:

Provides direction and focus: A digital marketing plan helps businesses define their goals, target audience, and messaging. By having a clear understanding of their objectives and target market, businesses can focus their resources and efforts on strategies that are most likely to drive results. This saves time and resources that could have been wasted on ineffective strategies.

Ensures consistency and cohesion: A digital marketing plan helps businesses ensure that their messaging and branding are consistent across all channels and platforms. This consistency helps build brand recognition and trust, and can ultimately lead to increased engagement and conversions. It also helps to establish a brand identity and a clear message that resonates with the target audience.

Enables measurement and optimization: By setting specific goals and KPIs, businesses can track and measure the effectiveness of their marketing efforts, and make informed decisions about how to optimize and improve their strategies for maximum ROI. This ensures that resources are allocated effectively, and that businesses are continuously improving their campaigns.

Helps allocate resources effectively: A digital marketing plan helps businesses allocate their resources (such as time, budget, and personnel) in a strategic and effective manner. By identifying the most effective strategies and channels, businesses can allocate their resources accordingly and maximize their impact. This also ensures that resources are not wasted on ineffective strategies.

Allows for agility and adaptability: A digital marketing plan is not set in stone; it should be flexible and adaptable to changes in the market and audience behavior. By regularly reviewing and adjusting their plan, businesses can stay agile and responsive to changes in the digital landscape. This allows them to pivot and adjust their strategies as needed to meet changing customer needs and preferences.

Another important reason why having a digital marketing plan is crucial for small businesses is that it helps to establish a clear understanding of the target audience. A digital marketing plan outlines the specific demographics, behaviors, and preferences of the target audience, which helps businesses create tailored messaging and campaigns that resonate with them.

Furthermore, having a digital marketing plan helps businesses stay ahead of the competition. With a well-defined plan, businesses can identify their unique selling proposition (USP) and leverage it to differentiate themselves from their competitors. This USP can be highlighted in their messaging and campaigns, and can help to attract and retain customers.

Having a digital marketing plan also helps businesses stay organized and on track. It outlines specific deadlines, milestones, and checkpoints that help businesses stay accountable and ensure that they are making progress towards their goals. This also helps to avoid distractions or tangents that can pull businesses away from their primary objectives.

Finally, having a digital marketing plan helps businesses to prioritize their efforts and avoid overextending themselves. With so many different digital channels and strategies available, it can be tempting for businesses to try to do everything at once. However, this can quickly become overwhelming and result in a lack of focus and direction. By having a well-defined plan, businesses can identify the most effective channels and strategies for their goals and allocate their resources accordingly.

In conclusion, having a digital marketing plan is essential for small businesses looking to succeed in today's digital marketplace. It helps to establish a clear understanding of the target audience, stay ahead of the competition, stay organized and on track, and prioritize efforts effectively. With a well-crafted plan, businesses can maximize their impact and drive results.

Setting objectives and goals

Setting objectives and goals is a critical component of any digital marketing plan. Objectives and goals provide direction and purpose to the plan and help businesses determine what they want to achieve. Here's why setting objectives and goals is important:

Provides clarity: Objectives and goals provide clarity about what the business wants to achieve through its digital marketing efforts. It helps businesses to define their purpose, and focus their resources and efforts on strategies that are most likely to achieve their objectives.

Measures success: Objectives and goals help businesses to measure the success of their digital marketing efforts. They provide a benchmark for businesses to evaluate the effectiveness of their strategies and tactics, and determine whether they are making progress towards achieving their objectives.

Enables focus: Objectives and goals help businesses to prioritize their efforts and focus on what matters most. They help businesses to avoid distractions and stay on track towards achieving their objectives.

Provides motivation: Objectives and goals can provide motivation and inspiration for businesses. They help to create a sense of purpose and direction, and can inspire businesses to take action and make progress towards achieving their objectives.

When setting objectives and goals, it's important to ensure they are SMART: specific, measurable, achievable, relevant, and time-bound. This means that objectives and goals should be:

Specific: Clearly defined and specific, so that everyone involved knows exactly what they are working towards.

Measurable: Able to be measured and tracked, so that progress can be monitored and evaluated.

Achievable: Realistic and achievable, so that businesses can be confident they can attain their objectives.

Relevant: Aligned with the overall business goals and relevant to the target audience.

Time-bound: Set within a specific timeframe, so that businesses have a deadline and can stay on track towards achieving their objectives.

In summary, setting objectives and goals is an important step in creating a digital marketing plan. They provide clarity, measure success, enable focus, and provide motivation. When setting objectives and goals, it's important to ensure they are SMART, so that businesses can be confident they are working towards achievable objectives that will help them achieve their overall business goals.

Developing a budget

Developing a budget is a crucial step in creating an effective digital marketing plan. A well-planned and well-executed budget can help businesses to maximize their return on investment (ROI) and achieve their marketing goals while staying within their financial limits.

One of the key benefits of developing a budget is that it provides financial discipline for businesses. By tracking their expenses and prioritizing their spending, businesses can avoid overspending and ensure that they are making the most of their available resources. A budget also helps businesses to be accountable for their spending, which is essential for long-term financial health.

Another important benefit of developing a budget is that it ensures ROI. By setting realistic goals and expectations, businesses can track their spending and measure the impact of their digital marketing efforts. This helps businesses to identify what is working and what is not, and to adjust their spending accordingly. By focusing on channels and strategies that generate a positive ROI, businesses can increase their profitability and competitiveness.

In addition to providing financial discipline and ensuring ROI, a budget allows businesses to experiment with different digital marketing channels and strategies. By allocating a portion of their budget to testing new channels and strategies, businesses can identify what works and what doesn't and adjust their spending accordingly. This helps businesses to stay competitive and keep up with changes in the market.

When developing a budget for digital marketing, businesses should consider a variety of factors. These include their marketing goals and objectives, their target audience, past performance, competition, and resource constraints. By taking these factors into account, businesses can create a budget that is tailored to their specific needs and goals.

Once a budget has been developed, it is important to monitor and adjust it as needed. This is because digital marketing is constantly evolving, and what worked in the past may not work as well in the future. By regularly reviewing and adjusting their budget, businesses can ensure that they are making the most of their resources and staying ahead of the competition.

Monitoring and adjusting a budget involves tracking key performance indicators (KPIs) and making data-driven decisions. By analyzing metrics such as website traffic, conversion rates, and customer acquisition costs, businesses can identify areas for improvement and make changes to their budget accordingly. This might involve shifting resources to more effective channels, adjusting ad targeting or messaging, or experimenting with new strategies.

In addition to monitoring and adjusting their budget, businesses should also track their ROI. This involves calculating the revenue generated by their digital marketing efforts and comparing it to the cost of those efforts. By regularly tracking their ROI, businesses can identify which channels and strategies are generating the most revenue and adjust their spending accordingly.

Overall, having a digital marketing plan with a well-developed budget is essential for small businesses to succeed in today's digital landscape. By setting clear objectives, developing a budget that supports those objectives, monitoring and adjusting the budget as needed, and tracking ROI, businesses can make the most of their digital marketing efforts and achieve their marketing goals.

Creating a timeline and action plan

Creating a timeline and action plan is an essential part of developing a digital marketing strategy. It involves setting a schedule for when specific tasks and activities will be completed, as well as identifying who will be responsible for each task. By creating a timeline and action plan, businesses can ensure that they stay on track and meet their marketing objectives.

One of the key benefits of creating a timeline and action plan is that it helps to break down larger goals into smaller, more manageable tasks. This makes it easier for businesses to stay organized and focused, and helps to ensure that each task is completed on time and to a high standard.

To create a timeline and action plan, businesses should start by identifying their key marketing objectives and then breaking these down into smaller, more specific goals. They should then identify the tasks and activities that will need to be completed in order to achieve these goals, and estimate how long each task will take.

Once the tasks have been identified and estimated, businesses should create a timeline that outlines when each task will be completed. This timeline should be realistic and take into account any resource constraints or other factors that might impact the completion of tasks.

In addition to creating a timeline, businesses should also assign responsibility for each task. This ensures that everyone involved in the marketing strategy knows what is expected of them and can work together effectively to achieve the desired results.

Regularly reviewing and updating the timeline and action plan is also important. As the marketing strategy progresses, businesses may need to adjust their timeline or make changes to the tasks that need to be completed. By regularly reviewing and updating the timeline, businesses can ensure that they stay on track and achieve their marketing objectives.

In addition to breaking down larger goals into smaller tasks and activities, creating a timeline and action plan can also help businesses to prioritize their marketing efforts. By identifying which tasks need to be completed first and allocating resources accordingly, businesses can focus on the most important and impactful activities, which can help to maximize their return on investment.

Creating a timeline and action plan can also improve collaboration and communication among team members. By assigning responsibility for each task and setting deadlines, team members can work together more effectively and avoid misunderstandings or duplication of effort. This can help to streamline the marketing process and ensure that everyone is working towards the same goals.

Finally, having a timeline and action plan can also help businesses to track their progress and measure their success. By monitoring the completion of tasks and activities, businesses can gain insights into what is working well and what needs improvement. They can also identify any areas where they may be falling behind schedule and make adjustments as needed to ensure that they stay on track.

In conclusion, creating a timeline and action plan is a critical step in developing a successful digital marketing strategy. By breaking down larger goals into smaller, more manageable tasks, prioritizing marketing efforts, improving collaboration and communication, and tracking progress and success, businesses can ensure that they stay on track and achieve their marketing objectives.

Chapter 12: Best practices for small business digital marketing

Consistency in branding and messaging

Consistency in branding and messaging is a key factor in building a strong and recognizable brand. It involves ensuring that all marketing materials, including logos, slogans, messaging, and imagery, are consistent across all channels and touchpoints.

When businesses maintain consistency in their branding and messaging, it helps to establish a clear identity and build trust with their target audience. Customers are more likely to remember and recognize a brand that has a consistent look and feel, and they are more likely to view it as reliable and trustworthy.

To achieve consistency in branding and messaging, businesses should start by defining their brand identity and ensuring that all marketing materials align with it. This includes developing a clear and concise brand message that communicates the unique value proposition of the business and resonates with the target audience.

Once the brand message has been established, businesses should ensure that it is consistently communicated across all channels and touchpoints, including their website, social media profiles, advertising, and other marketing materials. This can be achieved by using consistent branding elements, such as a consistent color scheme, font, and imagery.

Consistency in branding and messaging can also be achieved through regular monitoring and review of all marketing materials. This can help to identify any inconsistencies or areas where the brand message may be unclear or ineffective. By regularly reviewing and refining marketing materials, businesses can ensure that they stay on track and maintain consistency in their branding and messaging over time.

In addition to establishing a consistent brand identity and building trust with customers, consistency in branding and messaging can also help businesses to differentiate themselves from competitors. By maintaining a unique and consistent look and feel, businesses can stand out in a crowded market and establish themselves as leaders in their industry.

Consistency in branding and messaging can also improve the effectiveness of marketing efforts. When customers encounter consistent messaging across multiple touchpoints, they are more likely to develop a clear understanding of the business and its offerings. This can help to increase brand awareness, drive customer engagement, and ultimately lead to higher conversion rates.

Furthermore, consistency in branding and messaging can help businesses to build a loyal customer base. When customers encounter consistent messaging and branding, they are more likely to develop a sense of trust and loyalty towards the business. This can lead to repeat business, positive reviews, and referrals to new customers.

However, it's important to note that consistency in branding and messaging is not a one-time effort. It requires ongoing attention and monitoring to ensure that marketing materials remain consistent and aligned with the brand message over time. Regular review and refinement of marketing materials can help businesses to maintain consistency and ensure that their messaging remains effective and impactful.

In conclusion, consistency in branding and messaging is a critical element of a successful digital marketing strategy. It can help businesses to differentiate themselves from competitors, improve the effectiveness of marketing efforts, build a loyal customer base, and ultimately drive business growth. By defining a clear brand message, using consistent branding elements, and regularly reviewing and refining marketing materials, businesses can establish a consistent identity and build trust and loyalty with their target audience.

Staying up-to-date with trends and technologies

Staying up-to-date with trends and technologies is crucial in digital marketing. The digital landscape is constantly evolving, with new technologies and trends emerging regularly. To stay ahead of the competition, businesses must be aware of these changes and adapt their marketing strategies accordingly.

One of the primary benefits of staying up-to-date with trends and technologies is the ability to identify new opportunities for reaching and engaging with customers. For example, the rise of social media platforms and influencer marketing has created new channels for businesses to connect with their target audience. By staying informed about these trends and technologies, businesses can identify new opportunities to reach their customers and build their brand.

Staying up-to-date with trends and technologies can also help businesses to improve their marketing effectiveness. For example, the use of artificial intelligence and machine learning can help businesses to personalize their marketing efforts and improve the targeting of their campaigns. By incorporating these technologies into their digital marketing strategies, businesses can improve their ROI and drive better results.

Furthermore, staying up-to-date with trends and technologies can help businesses to future-proof their marketing efforts. By remaining agile and adaptable, businesses can quickly respond to changes in the market and take advantage of emerging opportunities. This can help businesses to stay relevant and competitive in the long run.

However, staying up-to-date with trends and technologies requires a significant investment of time and resources. Businesses must commit to ongoing learning and professional development to ensure that they remain informed and up-to-date. This may involve attending industry conferences, participating in online courses and webinars, or engaging with industry thought leaders and influencers.

To ensure that their digital marketing efforts are effective and relevant, businesses must prioritize staying up-to-date with trends and technologies. This involves continuously learning about new technologies, marketing channels, and consumer behaviors.

One way businesses can stay up-to-date with trends and technologies is by engaging with industry thought leaders and influencers. These individuals often have a deep understanding of the latest trends and developments in the industry and can provide valuable insights and advice. Businesses can follow these influencers on social media, attend their webinars and events, and read their blogs and articles to stay informed.

Attending industry conferences and events is another effective way to stay up-to-date with trends and technologies. These events bring together industry experts and thought leaders to discuss the latest developments and trends in the industry. By attending these events, businesses can gain valuable insights and network with other professionals in the field.

Another way to stay up-to-date is by participating in online courses and webinars. Many organizations offer online courses and webinars that cover topics such as digital marketing, social media marketing, and content marketing. These courses and webinars are a convenient way for businesses to stay informed and up-to-date while also improving their skills and knowledge.

In addition to these strategies, businesses must also prioritize ongoing learning and professional development. This means committing to a continuous learning mindset and actively seeking out new information and insights. By making learning a priority, businesses can stay ahead of the curve and ensure that their marketing efforts remain effective and relevant.

In conclusion, staying up-to-date with trends and technologies is essential for businesses that want to succeed in digital marketing. By engaging with industry thought leaders and influencers, attending industry conferences and events, participating in online courses and webinars, and prioritizing ongoing learning and professional development, businesses can stay informed and up-to-date with the latest developments in the industry.

Engaging with customers and responding to feedback

Engaging with customers and responding to their feedback is crucial for businesses that want to build strong relationships with their audience and improve their digital marketing efforts. By engaging with customers, businesses can gain valuable insights into their needs and preferences, which can help them tailor their marketing messages and offerings to better meet those needs.

One effective way to engage with customers is through social media. Businesses can use social media platforms to listen to what their customers are saying, respond to questions and comments, and share relevant content. By actively engaging with customers on social media, businesses can build trust and loyalty, which can lead to increased brand awareness and sales.

Another effective way to engage with customers is through email marketing. Businesses can use email to send personalized messages and promotions to their customers, which can help build loyalty and encourage repeat purchases. By tracking email metrics such as open rates and click-through rates, businesses can gain insights into the effectiveness of their campaigns and make adjustments as needed.

Responding to customer feedback is also crucial for businesses that want to improve their digital marketing efforts. By listening to what customers are saying and addressing their concerns, businesses can improve their products and services, as well as their marketing messages. This can lead to increased customer satisfaction and loyalty, which can ultimately lead to increased sales and revenue.

One effective way to gather customer feedback is through surveys and polls. By asking customers to provide feedback on their experiences with a business, businesses can gain valuable insights into what they are doing well and what they need to improve. By using this feedback to make improvements, businesses can show customers that they are committed to providing the best possible experience, which can build trust and loyalty.

Furthermore, engaging with customers and responding to their feedback also provides businesses with opportunities to create a positive image and reputation. When customers feel heard and valued, they are more likely to share their positive experiences with others. This can lead to increased word-of-mouth marketing, which is a powerful tool for small businesses.

Additionally, engaging with customers and responding to their feedback can help businesses identify areas for improvement. By listening to what customers are saying, businesses can identify common issues or pain points and make changes to their products, services, or marketing messages accordingly. This can help businesses stay competitive and relevant in their industry, and ensure that they are meeting the changing needs of their customers.

Another benefit of engaging with customers and responding to their feedback is that it can help businesses avoid negative reviews or customer complaints. By proactively addressing customer concerns and issues, businesses can prevent them from escalating and turning into negative reviews or social media posts. This can help maintain a positive image and reputation for the business, and can help attract new customers.

In summary, engaging with customers and responding to their feedback is an essential component of a successful digital marketing strategy for small businesses. By using social media and email marketing to engage with customers, gathering and responding to customer feedback, and using customer feedback to make improvements, businesses can build trust and loyalty, create a positive image and reputation, identify areas for improvement, and avoid negative reviews or customer complaints. All of these benefits can ultimately lead to increased sales and revenue for the business.

Continuous testing and optimization.

Continuous testing and optimization is an important aspect of digital marketing for small businesses. Essentially, it involves constantly analyzing and improving marketing campaigns and strategies based on data and feedback. By continually testing and optimizing, businesses can improve the effectiveness of their marketing efforts, which can ultimately lead to increased sales and revenue.

One key aspect of continuous testing and optimization is A/B testing. This involves creating two versions of a marketing campaign or website, and testing them to see which one performs better. For example, a business might create two versions of an email marketing campaign, with different subject lines, and send them to two different groups of customers. By tracking the open and click-through rates for each campaign, the business can determine which version was more effective, and use that information to improve future campaigns.

Another important aspect of continuous testing and optimization is using analytics to track the performance of marketing campaigns and identify areas for improvement. By monitoring metrics like website traffic, conversion rates, and social media engagement, businesses can identify which campaigns are working well and which ones need improvement. This can help businesses make data-driven decisions about how to allocate their marketing budget and resources.

In addition to A/B testing and analytics, continuous testing and optimization also involves constantly experimenting with new strategies and tactics. This can include trying out new social media platforms, testing different ad formats, or experimenting with new types of content. By constantly pushing the boundaries and trying new things, businesses can stay ahead of the competition and keep their marketing efforts fresh and engaging.

Another important benefit of continuous testing and optimization is that it allows businesses to be more agile and responsive to changing market conditions. In today's fast-paced digital landscape, trends and consumer behaviors can change rapidly. By continually testing and optimizing their marketing strategies, businesses can quickly adapt to these changes and stay ahead of the curve.

For example, if a social media platform that a business relies on for marketing suddenly loses popularity, the business can quickly pivot and shift their focus to a new platform that is gaining traction. By staying agile and adaptable, businesses can ensure that their marketing efforts remain effective and relevant, even as market conditions change.

Finally, continuous testing and optimization can help businesses avoid wasted time and resources on ineffective marketing strategies. By continually monitoring and optimizing campaigns, businesses can quickly identify and eliminate strategies that are not generating results, and focus their efforts on those that are. This can help businesses save money and resources, and ultimately drive more efficient and effective marketing campaigns.

Overall, continuous testing and optimization is a critical component of a successful digital marketing strategy for small businesses. By constantly analyzing and improving marketing campaigns based on data and feedback, businesses can stay competitive, drive growth and revenue, and remain agile and adaptable in an ever-changing market.

Chapter 13: Conclusion

Recap of the importance of digital marketing for small businesses

Digital marketing is crucial for small businesses as it provides a range of benefits and advantages that can help them grow and succeed in today's competitive market. One of the main advantages of digital marketing is that it is cost-effective and provides a level playing field for small businesses to compete with larger businesses. This is because digital marketing channels such as social media, email, and search engines do not discriminate based on company size, allowing small businesses to reach a wider audience and build their brand.

Another benefit of digital marketing for small businesses is that it allows them to target specific audiences based on demographics, interests, and behaviors. This targeted approach ensures that businesses are reaching the right people with their marketing messages, increasing the chances of conversion and generating a positive return on investment (ROI).

Digital marketing also provides real-time data and analytics that allow businesses to track the effectiveness of their marketing campaigns. This information can be used to continually improve and optimize marketing strategies to ensure that they are achieving the desired results.

Moreover, digital marketing enables small businesses to establish a strong online presence, which is essential in today's digital landscape. By leveraging various digital marketing strategies such as SEO, social media marketing, email marketing, PPC advertising, content marketing, influencer marketing, and affiliate marketing, small businesses can connect with customers, build trust and loyalty, and ultimately drive revenue.

In summary, digital marketing is a critical component of a successful business strategy for small businesses. By leveraging various digital marketing channels and techniques, small businesses can level the playing field, connect with customers, build their brand, and achieve their business goals.

Final thoughts and next steps

In conclusion, digital marketing is an essential tool for small businesses to compete in the modern marketplace. By understanding the various digital marketing strategies available and how they can benefit their business, small business owners can create effective marketing campaigns that reach their target audience and drive growth.

The next steps for small businesses looking to implement a digital marketing strategy would be to conduct research and analysis to identify their target audience, create customer personas, and develop a comprehensive digital marketing plan that includes goals, objectives, and a budget. It is also crucial to establish a strong online presence, develop engaging content, and use various digital marketing channels to promote products and services.

Continuous monitoring and optimization are also crucial to ensure that the digital marketing efforts are effective in achieving business goals. Regular review of metrics and data, testing different approaches, and adapting to changes in the market can help small businesses stay ahead of the competition and achieve success.

Overall, digital marketing can provide small businesses with the tools they need to reach a wider audience, build their brand, and grow their business. By investing in digital marketing strategies and staying up-to-date with the latest trends and technologies, small businesses can achieve their business goals and thrive in today's digital landscape.